TENNESSEE
TROUT WATERS
Blue-Ribbon Fly-Fishing Guide

Ian Rutter

TENNESSEE
TROUT WATERS
Blue-Ribbon Fly-Fishing Guide

Ian Rutter

Frank Amato
PORTLAND

Biography

Ian Rutter grew up in East Tennessee not far from the Great Smoky Mountains. He took up fly fishing when he attended the University of Tennessee at Knoxville, where he studied botany and zoology. Ian and his wife Charity operate R&R Fly Fishing Guide Service out of Townsend, Tennessee where they live in the shadow of the Smokies. They also contribute articles and photographs to a number of fly-fishing publications. You can find fishing reports for East Tennessee on Ian's website, www.randrflyfishing.com

Acknowledgments

I would like to thank my wife Charity for her constant encouragement and assistance on this project. I would also like to thank Chuck Robinson of the FlyChucker Fly Shop in Brentwood, Tennessee for his helpful insights on Middle Tennessee tailwaters. Thanks to Bruce Wankel at Virginia Creeper Fly Shop in Abingdon, Virginia for his advice on the South Holston and Watauga tailwaters. Last, but not least, I would like to thank my great friends Tim Doyle, Roy Hawk, Doug Sanders, Walter Babb, Andy Sonner, and Stan Smartt for always being ready to fish new waters and pose for photos.

Photography: Ian & Charity Rutter unless otherwise noted.
Map Illustrations: Ian Rutter
Design: Jerry Hutchinson & Charity Rutter
Cover Design: Charity Rutter

Softbound ISBN-13: 978-1-57188-294-3
Softbound UPC: 0-81127-00121-7

Frank Amato Publications, Inc.
P.O. Box 82112, Portland, Oregon 97282
(503) 653-8108
Printed in Singapore
3 5 7 9 10 8 6 4

Table of Contents

TENNESSEE
TROUT WATERS
Blue-Ribbon Fly Fishing Guide

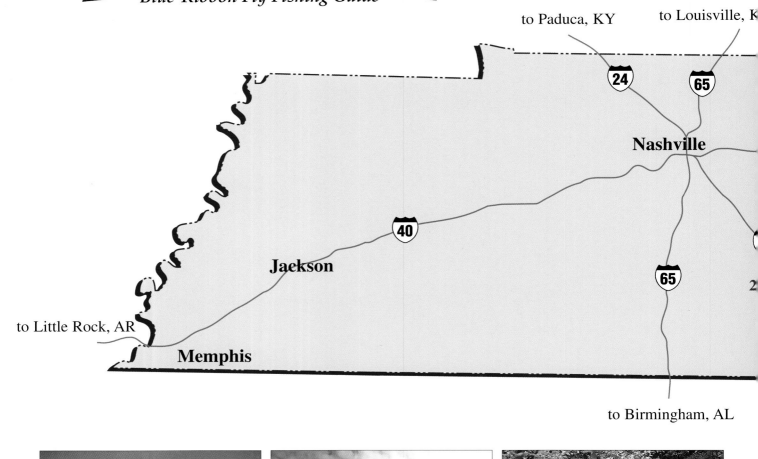

to Paduca, KY

to Louisville, K

Nashville

Jackson

to Little Rock, AR

Memphis

to Birmingham, AL

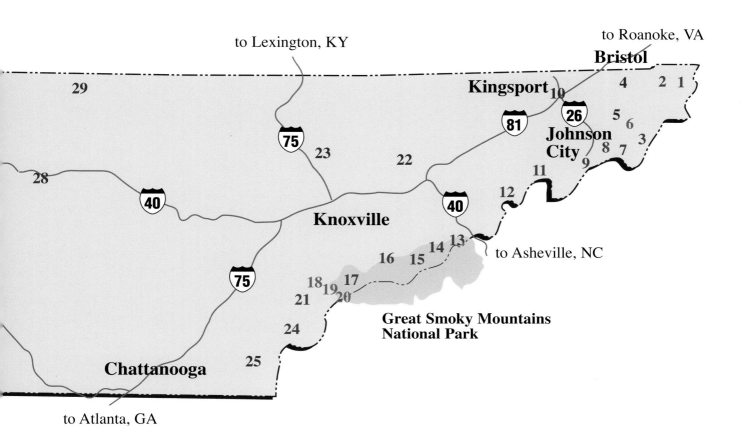

to Lexington, KY

to Roanoke, VA

Bristol

29

Kingsport 10

4   2 1

81

26

5   6

Johnson City

3

8 7

9

23

75

22

11

28

12

40

40

to Asheville, NC

Knoxville

14 13

16   15

18 19 17

75

20

21

Great Smoky Mountains National Park

24

Chattanooga

25

to Atlanta, GA

TAILWATERS
28   CANEY FORK
23   CLINCH RIVER
27   DUCK RIVER
26   ELK RIVER
10   FORT PATRICK HENRY TAILWATER
25   HIWASSEE RIVER
22   HOLSTON RIVER
29   OBEY RIVER
4   SOUTH HOLSTON RIVER
5   WATAUGA RIVER

TAILWATER LAKES
20   CALDERWOOD LAKE
19   CHILHOWEE LAKE
18   TELLICO LAKE
6   WILBUR LAKE

FREESTONE STREAMS & RIVERS
17   ABRAMS CREEK
2   BEAVERDAM CREEK
21   CITICO CREEK
13   COSBY CREEK
7   DOE RIVER
11   HORSE CREEK
1   LAUREL CREEK
3   LAUREL FORK
16   LITTLE RIVER
14   MIDDLE PRONG LITTLE PIGEON RIVER
8   NORTH INDIAN CREEK
12   PAINT CREEK
9   SOUTH INDIAN CREEK
24   TELLICO RIVER
15   WEST PRONG LITTLE PIGEON RIVER

Introduction
Tennessee Fly Water

A fly-fisherman puts his waders on only a few yards from the river. The cold temperatures of the tailwater conflict with the warm, humid atmosphere and create a thick fog over the water. There are so many rise dimples on the water that at first glance it seems that a light rain is falling. The fisherman ties on a tiny midge emerger but is biding his time for the big hatch this afternoon. Hopefully there will be a good hatch of sulphurs to bring even the largest fish to the surface to feed. This is the best month of the year to find a good trout feeding aggressively.

At the exact same moment, about an hour's drive away, another fisherman prepares for his day on the water. He is parked at a trailhead that follows a mountain stream. He has left his waders at home and is packing his felt-bottom boots in a small backpack with his water bottle and lunch. His fly box is full of bushy dry flies. He got his fill of nymph fishing last winter and doesn't plan to fish with anything but Stimulators, Wulffs, and Parachutes today. Most of the trout he will catch will be small, but he will rack up some numbers. The biggest reason he fishes here is because he normally only shares the stream with a few fishermen on any day.

Yet a third fly-fisherman has begun his day on the water. He launched his small johnboat in the lake at first light. His chances of catching trout will plummet once the sun gets on the water. Like the other two fishermen he is also looking forward to rising trout. However, he will not match the numbers of trout the small-stream fisherman will. Nor will he have the consistency the tailwater fisherman can expect. The best day he can ever remember having on the lake was five trout brought to the boat. However, the smallest of the five trout was sixteen inches. He has been skunked far more often than the other two fishermen.

These three fishermen are fishing at the same time on a hypothetical morning. However, none of these fishermen are more than a two-hour drive from each other, and are possibly closer. The state of Tennessee is rarely given credit for its sheer volume of trout waters. Even those who acknowledge its prominent waters rarely recognize the variety of trout-fishing experiences that are available. A Tennessee fly fisherman has to travel a long distance to find trout fisheries as good and as varied as his home waters.

When I began trout fishing some years ago I was fairly naive in my approach to the trout rivers and streams close to my home in east Tennessee. I might spend Saturday morning on the Clinch River tailrace below Norris Dam and Sunday on a mountain stream like Little River or Tellico River. During that initial period of wrestling with a fly rod, my methods and flies differed little between the mountain streams and tailwaters. Later as I learned more and met more trout fishermen, my whole approach changed. I eventually came to realize that while both the freestone streams and tailwaters held trout, they were not much alike.

Most of the tailwaters in Tennessee have a relatively constant water temperature throughout the year. There is some fluctuation but you can usually be assured that the water will be very cold. The freestone streams are different, warming throughout spring with a few becoming marginal for trout during the hottest days of a summer drought.

Freestone streams maintain a relatively constant flow from one day to the next. Sudden downpours of rain can raise their level in a short time, but barring any heavy rains their water level will vary only slightly day to day. The tailwaters will have dramatically different water flows in a matter of minutes. Sometimes you may find several fishermen gathering by the river, collecting their flies and putting their waders on. All the while, an unfamiliar fisherman might look at these fellows wondering where they might plan to wade since the river is not only swift, but several feet deep. Once their rods are assembled and they're ready to go, it's as if Moses had taken up trout fishing. The river falls to an easy level to wade and trout begin to rise as insects emerge en masse. Hours later, these same fishermen will seemingly decide they've had enough and reel up the slack in their line and put their gear away just minutes before the river rises several feet. While periods of generation may differ at different times of year, TVA posts generation schedules so you can duplicate the same feat safely.

Trout lakes in Tennessee are extremely different from many lakes in the Rocky Mountains. These lakes are actually impoundments on river systems regulated by TVA dams. Like the tailwater rivers, these lakes have a relatively stable temperature and their levels may fluctuate radically over the course of a day. These lakes are relatively small and often feature some current. You will not find lakes that hold trout any further south.

As my enthusiasm for fly fishing grew with my greed for more trout, I traveled to other parts of the country. The rivers of Wyoming, Montana, and Idaho were a lure I could not resist. However, to my amazement, fishermen of these famous rivers were curious about the streams and rivers I had just left. I found that the tremendous diversity of tailwater rivers, mountains streams, and lakes of my home was an exceptionally rare combination over a relatively small landscape. Much of this water is on public land as well. One August when a friend of mine visited the Henry's Fork in Idaho, he found a transplanted Tennessean pining for home. "Yeah, the Fork's good, but I tell you what... the South Holston's better."

The intention of this book is to give the reader a good starting point for exploring the trout waters of Tennessee. The different waters are divided into three separate sections: tailwaters, mountain freestone streams, and lakes. The information contained in this book should give any fisherman a good starting point to visit any of these streams for the first time. The best areas to float or wade are given, as well as seasonal considerations. Maps are provided to help you get your bearings.

Dedicated trout fishermen might also consult a few other publications before taking to the stream. A copy of *Tennessee Atlas & Gazetteer* by DeLorme is indespensible for driving around on back roads. Those who plan to fish in the backcountry might also pick up copies of *Wilderness Trails of Tennessee's Cherokee National Forest* and *Hiking Trails of the Smokies*. Both of these books provide excellent descriptions of the trails in Tennessee's wild lands. *Great Smoky Mountains National Park Angler's Companion* is a fly-fishing guide I wrote which provides more information on the streams in the Smokies.

Quick Reference Symbols

Next to the name of individual trout waters you will find a set of icons that can provide a quick synopsis of what that body of water has to offer. There are icons for each species of trout you are likely to catch, roadside access, walk-in access, backcountry camping opportunities, and developed campgrounds. For more detailed information you should read the description. For instance, several streams will have icons for rainbows, brook, and brown trout. However, no stream will have all three trout throughout its length. You will find information in the description about where the trout occur in the stream.

Rainbow Trout

Brown Trout

Brook Trout

A significant portion of the stream may be fished along a road.

A significant portion of the stream may only be reached by hiking.

Backcountry camping is available at campsite on the stream.

Camping is available on or near this stream and is accessible by car.

These waters are fishable with a canoe. Canoes can help fishermen gain access to remote sections of rivers. They may not be the most stable platforms to use during generation on tailwaters. Personal pontoon craft are also serviceable in the same instances that canoes are.

A combination of current and depth makes these waters ideal to fish from a drift boat or raft. An anchor system is usually needed to hold over the best spots for an extended period.

Motorized boats may be used. These boats may not be the best craft to use in all rivers. They are, however, the best boats to use on the lakes.

SIZE 2

You will find this on the descriptions of freestone streams. They are rated in size of the stream, 1 being the smallest and 10 being the largest. Long streams will grow smaller as you go upstream so the largest ratings typically apply to downstream areas.

Tailwater Fishing

Tailwater fishing in Tennessee is distinctly different from fishing on the freestone mountain streams. The most obvious differences are that the tailwaters are much larger than the freestones and generation schedules have a direct effect on hatches and fishing access. Many fishermen prefer fishing the tailwaters because the fish are dramatically larger than they are in the freestone streams. They are also a bit less strenuous to fish. These rivers are also ideal for float fishing, something all together out of the question on small streams.

There are several reasons why the tailwaters produce larger trout than the natural freestone streams. First, and most obvious, they are far larger. Tailwater trout have a large river to grow in and have more freedom to feed and hide than if they were restricted to a few small pools in a creek.

Tailwater rivers also have water temperatures that are usually far more favorable for trout than the natural streams. Trout require water temperatures of seventy degrees or less, but do best when water temperatures are between fifty and sixty five. Most of the tailwaters maintain water temperatures in the low fifties throughout the year. Trout are cold blooded and their metabolism is directly affected by water temperature. The water temperature in these rivers is almost always within a trout's favored range and almost never gets high enough to get their metabolism very high. Many of the larger freestone streams will push the upper ends of the temperature tolerance during the summer. These high temperatures will raise a trout's metabolism and food demands. A trout with a lower metabolism can direct a larger proportion of its food intake to growth.

The third, and possibly most important, reason why trout grow larger in the tailwaters is because of the abundant food base. Most freestone streams in east Tennessee are not very fertile. The Appalachians are the oldest mountains in the world. There is very little mineral nutrition left in the soils that can be absorbed into the rivers. The only nutritive input is from falling leaves which break down on the stream bottom. This typically washes away on the currents, though. When dams were built on the Tennessee River system they essentially created large impoundments where much of the sediment from their tributaries settles to the bottom. As a result, water on the bottom of the lakes is extremely rich in dissolved minerals. This is the water that gets pulled through a dam's turbines. These dissolved minerals are the building blocks for life and are the components of cell walls in plants, exoskeletons on aquatic insects, and shells for crayfish and snails.

Drift boats are an excellent means of fishing many of Tennessee's tailwater rivers.

The biological differences between freestones and tailwaters are as different as the way the two are fished. For the most part, there can be no generation from the dam's powerhouse in order for wading to be possible. There are some exceptions to this rule, however. This will be described in more detail in each tailwater's respective section. With generation, several of the tailwaters remain fishable from a boat. Also, rising water takes time to travel downstream. There are many instances where you may be able to leave a location near the dam and travel some miles downstream and have several hours to fish before the water reaches you. In some cases, the generators may have stopped by the time the water reaches you and you can turn around and head back upstream. In most cases the water will move at about four river miles per hour. This is not a hard and fast rule, but it is often a good estimate. Water moves faster if two generators come on as opposed to only one. Straight, narrow rivers also rise faster than wider ones or those with many bends.

Rain can often drastically affect the fishing on freestone streams but it takes quite a bit of rain to change a dam's generation schedule. Schedules are often favorable for wading in the spring when the reservoirs are being filled. Generation in the summer often depends on rainfall amounts throughout the region. Dry years add up to less water available for generation. Excessive rainfall will require that the dams release water to keep certain areas from flooding. The dams will sometimes open flood gates and spill water in extreme cases. The period around Labor Day is when lakes begin to draw down to winter pool. This often keeps water flowing for several weeks to several months. There is usually plenty of down time in the winter for fishing. However, wet winters can keep generators pushing water. Late winter and spring are the times of heaviest precipitation in the Tennessee Valley. Lakes are generally kept low over the winter in preparation for the spring rains.

While there are many freestone streams with only wild-trout populations, every tailwater receives its share of stocked trout. Some of these trout are stocked as catchable—size fish. However, recent research has indicated that trout stocked into the tailwaters as fingerlings have a far better survival rate and are often the trout that reach trophy status. Most of the 9- to 12-inch trout that are stocked are caught relatively quickly. There is now a movement toward stocking more fingerlings and fewer catchables. Fingerlings seem to take to natural foods quicker than older trout. They also have to deal with predators. Those who graduate to adulthood have learned a few survival tricks. Also, since fingerlings require less time in a hatchery, more trout can be stocked at less expense.

Tailwater trout do not seem to live in the perpetual fear that their mountain cousins do. A delicate presentation and careful wading are always important. However, these fish are pretty forgiving. Also, it's not uncommon for fishermen to fish the same run for several hours without a break in the action. I remember fishing the South Holston one afternoon with Brian Courtney. I stalked my way up and down the runs all afternoon, picking up a few nice trout. Brian, on the other hand, pulled up a stool on one nice run and milked it the whole time. He would catch several trout over a period of thirty minutes or so. If he went more than ten minutes without a strike, he'd change flies and start hooking up. Rather than change locations, he chose to change flies. This technique might work through one or two cycles in the mountain streams but certainly not all day long.

Fly fishermen everywhere attach importance to fly selection. This is one department where diligence pays dividends on the tailwaters. Most of the water in these rivers is relatively flat and slow. You can count on exceptional clarity. Very few fish will succumb to generic attractor patterns and there is a reason for this. All of the tailwaters have rich aquatic food bases. However, most of them are somewhat limited in diversity. The Clinch River, for example, is full of midges, scuds, sow bugs, and sulphur mayflies. These foods are virtually the only items trout eat here. Large stonefly nymphs produce well in the mountain streams where those nymphs are common. However, since they are absent in most of the tailwaters, trout will not recognize them as food. This is much the same as people in Japan who have grown up eating sushi and think nothing of it. Many Americans, on the other hand, are relatively new to this type of food and just can't bring themselves to eat raw fish.

Tailwater fishermen typically fish nymph patterns. Dry flies have their moments, particularly on those rivers with good mayfly and caddis populations. However, tiny midges make up a significant part of a trout's diet in most of these rivers. That also means that smaller patterns will often outfish larger ones. Most tailwater fly fishermen consider a size-16 fly relatively large. Flies in size 18-22 are often the norm. Small hooks also means fine tippets. A 6X tippet is average when fishing such small flies. You will probably find spools of 7X and 8X in a lot of fishing vests. Fluorocarbon tippet is less visible than monofilament and widely used since water conditions are generally clear and slow.

Many anglers consider the mountain streams to be far more strenuous to wade than tailwater rivers. This is true, mostly because the tailwater fishermen can set up shop on a good run and not move far. However, wading can be every bit as treacherous on these large rivers as it is on the boulder-lined freestones. Muddy banks are a staple on the tailwaters and you are likely to slide down a few if you spend much time on them. Slow water tends to lull waders into a false sense of complacency, but algae-coated rocks can drop you in an instant. These larger rivers also have a number of submerged ledges that go from only one or two feet deep to five feet or deeper. Remember the old proverb that still waters run deep. Many fishermen consider cleats to be a valuable addition to the felt on their boots.

Ask a biologist what a trout's top requirement is and he'll tell you 'cold water'. All of the tailwaters have it. Water comes from the bottom of the lake where it's the coldest and travels through the turbines into the river bed. In many instances, water temperatures in the river will be in the low fifties or high forties even in the middle of the summer. This also has an effect on the air temperature in the river bed. This means that fishermen have to dress accordingly. If you show up at the crack of dawn, you should probably dress in layers. The cold water will chill the air for a few feet above the surface. This can create the signature tailwater fog on warm, humid days. It might be seventy degrees as you don your waders in the dim light of morning. However, the damp, foggy air over the river will be noticeably cooler. This is not a big issue as long as you don't wear lightweight waders over shorts. Lightweight waders are definitely better than neoprenes in the summer, and will serve you well during the winter with appropriate insulation underneath. Rainy days are always chilly on the tailwaters. There is no sun to warm hands that get dunked in the icy water. Rain jackets should definitely be brought along. The chill is not as noticeable when you're dry.

Generation schedules are usually posted by 5:00 p.m. the day before but there are several things to keep in mind. TVA and the Army Corps of Engineers both reserve the right to change the schedule. If you get the schedule the night before, it is always a good idea to check before you leave in the morning. A schedule change can affect your location and the amount of time you have to fish. Depending on where you are, it is a good idea to check the schedules of several rivers so you have an alternate plan. It is rare for a schedule to change without 6-8 hours notice but it does happen. Practically every fisherman that has spent a few years on Tennessee's tailwaters has had his fishing cut short by rising water he didn't expect.

Tailwater fishermen should exercise a fair bit of paranoia when it comes to rising water. Try to keep an eye on an exposed rock or place on the river bank and check on it often. Rising water is fairly obvious if you're close to the dam. If you happen to be several miles downstream, water rises rather discreetly. By the time you notice the rising water it may be too late for you to get back to the bank without swimming. Be aware of debris floating down the river. Rising water will pick up any leaves and twigs that have fallen.

Another common scenario is that you might have fished several hours with only a handful of missed strikes. Suddenly your strike indicator goes under and you pull in the first fish of the day. The very next cast also hooks up. "It's about time," you think to yourself as you look at your watch. The water is due to come up at any time and you were afraid that you'd leave with the skunk on your back. After releasing another nice fish you eagerly cast back into the run and the fly barely drifts six feet before it is taken. This trout races downstream. "Hmmm....This is a better fish," you think to yourself. "He sure has some pull. In fact, he's pulling so hard he's taking me with him!" The current is pushing hard against you and the water is only inches from the top of your waders.

Rising water dislodges food in the river and brings on a sudden feeding frenzy. Fishermen are often so distracted by the flurry of activity, they don't realize what is going on. Experienced tailwater fishermen often realize what is going on, but still can't tear themselves from the river before it's too late. I've heard of one fisherman that puts a $20 bill on dry river bottom near the bank. His frugal nature keeps him from letting the cash float away and brings him to safety.

This can also be good information for fishermen that are floating the river. A boat that can stay with the surge of rising water can experience some excellent fishing. It can be pretty tough to stay with the initial surge so it is more practical to have your boat positioned in a favorite spot when the water does rise.

Tailwater Information

The most useful information any fisherman can have before heading out to a tailwater is the generation schedules. These schedules are usually posted on the Internet or recorded messages may be obtained by phone. Most of the time, these schedules can be obtained the evening before. However, these schedules may change. Schedules are usually accurate for several hours. Changes are most likely to occur overnight.

Past releases are just as important as scheduled releases later in the day. Learning what the water releases have been for the past few hours can help you plan your day around rising or falling water. Even though generators may not be running at the moment, water may not have yet fallen at points downstream. In fact, low water downstream may still rise if a previous release has not yet traveled that far.

The Tennessee Valley Authority posts generation schedules and predicted flows on their website and they also have a toll-free number with recorded information. After calling their phone number you will be given a number of choices. Selecting 4 will take you to the generation schedules and you will be asked to dial the two-digit number of the dam in which you are interested.

The website will give you more information in an easier-to-use format. You can also obtain predicted river flows for the next three days. This can also be helpful for planning a trip. If flows are optimal today and the average flow over the next couple of days is identical to today, chances are excellent that generation schedules will be similar. However, if predicted flows are dramatically higher over the next few days you can bet that more water will be generated. Similarly, if generation doesn't allow fishing today, check to see what the predicted flows are for the next few days. If they are dramatically reduced flows, expect better generation schedules for fishing.

The following is a list of numbers and Internet addresses where you can obtain critical tailwater release information. Tennessee Valley Authority Lakes & Rivers site: **lakeinfo.tva.gov/**
US Army Corps of Engineers Lake & Fishing information site. This site only has information concerning Corps of Engineers Dams. The only ones that are applicable for trout tailwaters in Tennessee are the Caney Fork and Obey River.
www.orn.usace.army.mil/pao/lakeinfo/fishinginfo.html

TVA Lake & River Information Line: 800-238-2264

Caney Fork Tailwater/Center Hill Dam	**#37**
Clinch River/Norris Dam	**#17**
Duck River/Normandy Dam	**#56**
Elk River/Tim's Ford Dam	**#50**
Hiwassee River/Apalachia Dam	**#22**
Holston River/Cherokee Dam	**#05**
Obey River/Dale Hollow Dam	**#35**
South Holston River/South Holston Dam	**#01**
South Holston River/Fort Patrick Henry Dam	**#04**
Watauga River / Wilbur Dam	**#42**

The Caney Fork is among the most popular rivers in Tennessee. A large part of this river's popularity comes from the fact that this is one of the only quality trout fisheries near the metropolis of Nashville. Its cold flow originates below Center Hill Dam and heads for its confluence with the Cumberland River. For years the dissolved oxygen content in the river was fairly low, particularly in late summer and early fall. This limited the river's productivity. Following the TVA's example, the Army Corps of Engineers installed equipment in the turbines to increase dissolved oxygen in the water. This has led to more abundant aquatic food resources, carry over of stocked trout, and, in turn, larger fish.

There are very few pieces of broken water on the Caney. Most of the water is fairly slick and feeding lanes are formed by tongues of current. The flow is relatively slow when conditions allow for wading. However, do not be lulled into a false sense of security, when the Caney begins to rise it rises quickly. You can easily get caught on the wrong side of the river, or worse.

The Caney Fork is the most popular river in middle Tennessee.

Midges and caddis are the predominant trout foods in the Caney Fork. As a result, dry-fly fishing is probably the least productive method for hooking trout. Midges and caddis larvae are among the most popular imitations. While trout often appear to take midges off the surface, they are more likely to be sucking in emergers just under the surface. Soft-hackle fly patterns have also grown in popularity as caddis populations have increased. One of the most popular patterns on the river is the Eat at Chuck's. This purple soft-hackle comes from the vise of Chuck Robinson, a fly shop owner and guide in Brentwood. Another pattern found in fly boxes up and down the Caney is the Guacamole Stick. This is a bright-green imitation of a caddis larva tied with vernille. Woolly Buggers have always been a staple.

The Caney has always been a favorite of waders and drift fishermen in middle Tennessee. There are several public access points on the river and they are concentrated on the upper half of the river. Those who float the river will typically find a bit more solitude. Its gentle flow makes it an easy river to maneuver as long as the turbines are not generating. Water levels fluctuate dramatically with generation. Guides typically float the Caney Fork in drift boats but it is a prime candidate for those who can round up a canoe and use it for transportation to less-accessible runs. Canoes can even be rented at a small store near Edgar Evins State Park and Center Hill Dam. Be sure to get off the water before it rises though, since the water can rise as much as eight feet.

Most fishermen will get to the Caney via I-40. Exit at Buffalo Valley and Edgar Evins State Park for access to the dam and Happy Hollow. Taking the exit for Carthage and Gordonsville will get you on the lower sections of the river.

Wading
The furthest upstream access points are directly below Center Hill Dam. There are access points on either side of the

Wading the Caney at Happy Hollow.

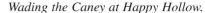

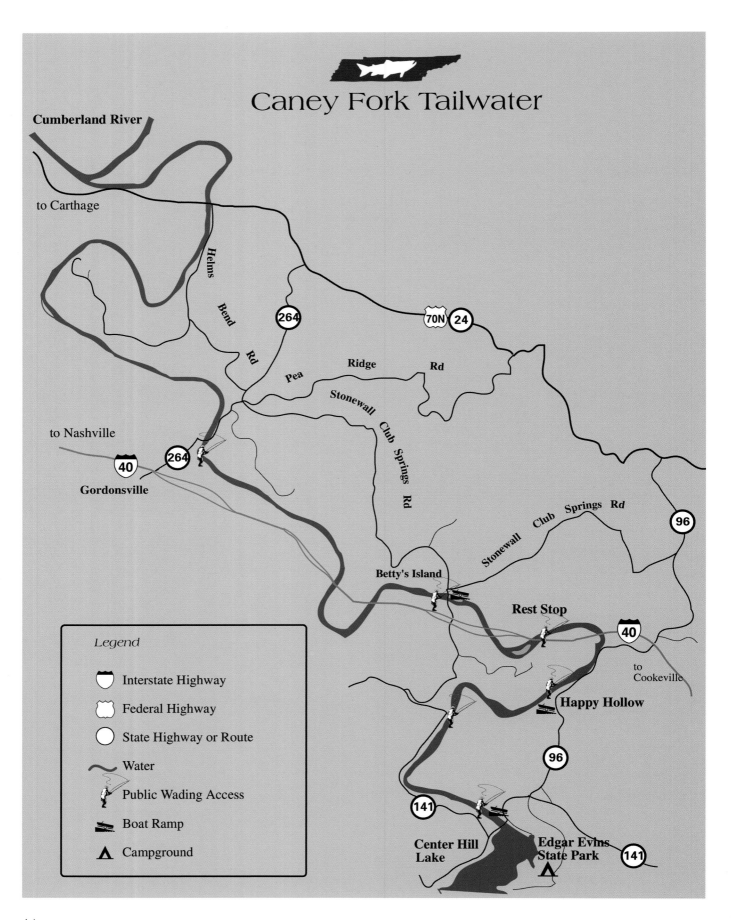

Caney Fork Tailwater

Cumberland River

to Carthage

Helms Bend Rd

264

70N 24

Pea Ridge Rd

Stonewall Club Springs Rd

to Nashville

40

264

Gordonsville

Stonewall Club Springs Rd

96

Betty's Island

Rest Stop

40

to Cookeville

Happy Hollow

96

Legend

Interstate Highway

Federal Highway

State Highway or Route

Water

Public Wading Access

Boat Ramp

Campground

141

Center Hill Lake

Edgar Evins State Park

141

dam. The access on the north/east side of the river has a boat ramp. Another access is only a few miles downstream. Know when the generator is scheduled to start. Water begins to rise as soon as the generators start pulling water.

The Lancaster access is on the west side of the Caney off TN 141. This is an unimproved access near the community of Lancaster. Rising water takes about 45 minutes to arrive here.

The next point downstream is Happy Hollow, probably the most popular access on the river. This is a TWRA access and the area is marked with a sign. Oftentimes wading fishermen will pull their vehicle right down into the river bed to set up. This is really a foolish move. This is not a good place to find you have a dead battery, or mire down in the river bed as the water gets deeper. Water begins to rise a little more than two hours after generation starts.

Perhaps the most overlooked access point is one of the most obvious. The I-40 rest area has plenty of parking and it is only a short walk to the water. In spite of the proximity to one of the nation's busiest roadways, this can sometimes be one of the more peaceful places to wade the river. There is plenty of room to walk upstream or down and find a nice spot to cast. Water begins to rise about two and a half hours after the turbines start pulling water.

Betty's Island is the next point down the river where you can find a place to park and fish. There is nearly a half mile of water that can be easily reached on foot. There is also a gravel bar here where fishermen sometimes park and tempt fate. This is one of the more crowded points on the river but there is usually enough room for everyone to spread out. Water will begin to rise a little over three hours after the generators come on.

Access is possible at a few bridges downstream of Betty's Island, but most of the river bank is actually on private property. Be sure to park on the state right of way.

Floating

The Caney Fork is most often floated from the dam down to Betty's Island. Drift boats and canoes can be used with ease provided Center Hill Dam isn't generating water. Flows are too swift to make float fishing practical. John boats might have

A Caney Fork rainbow heads home.

A quiet morning on the Caney Fork.

some use on the Caney but many places are a bit too shallow to have a prop hanging down when the water is off and the water is too swift to make fishing practical when it's on. Happy Hollow is not really a ramp when the water is down but I've seen popular ramps on other rivers far more difficult to access with a boat trailer. You can drive down into the river bed, just be sure to park your vehicle at the top of the hill.

Betty's Island is an easy spot to launch or recover anything up to the size of a drift boat. However, this is not a real ramp so check things out before you commit to anything. Canoes and pontoons will have no problem getting in or out of the water.

Canoes and pontoons are the only boats that can be pulled from the river near any of the bridges further downstream. Anything that requires a trailer should be ruled out. The interstate rest stop is a bit too far from the river to make carrying a canoe or pontoon anything but a drudge. There are sections of the Caney that lend themselves to a good float trip. The first is from the dam to Happy Hollow. The second is from Happy Hollow to Betty's Island. Both of these floats have good points to launch and recover boats and the distance is just about right for a good day of fishing. A float from the dam to Betty's Island is possible but you will need a lot of daylight. You might also spend more time traveling than fishing to make the Betty's Island take-out by dark.

Alternatives

The Caney Fork's relative isolation from other trout fisheries can just about end the day if generation schedules change unexpectedly once you've gotten to the river. It's always a good idea to check at the last minute even if you already know what the schedule is. Generation schedules are subject to change. Locals have come to expect this and will often check schedules one last time before getting in the water.

If you're in the area for an extended period and flows on the Caney don't allow fishing, look to the Elk and Duck rivers to the south. These small tailwaters are better than an hour from the Caney Fork but can provide fishing opportunities for the determined trout angler. Also check generation schedules on the Obey. This is north of the Caney and a bit closer than the Elk and Duck.

Tailwaters
Clinch River

Depending on the day you come to fish, the Clinch may be the most incredible trout fishing experience you've ever had, or one of the most frustrating. During the good times, some fishermen refer to the river as "The Cinch", but call it "The Grinch" during the tough times. The Clinch is the classic example of a Tennessee tailwater. Its water remains ice-cold all year long, and its trout grow with remarkable speed. While the food base is not particularly diverse, it is incredibly abundant. The menu for trout consists mostly of sow bugs, scuds, and midge larvae. Caddis and mayflies are present in the river, but their imitations do not have the day-to-day consistency of the sowbug and midge patterns.

The Clinch can be fished with a variety of flies, but the most productive fishers have a strong bias toward small nymphs and fine tippets. Many of the most successful flies are fished in a size 18 or smaller. Sulphur mayfly and midge hatches can often provide stellar examples of selective trout. The picky nature of Clinch River trout is legendary, and most of the regulars fish their own jealously-guarded fly patterns. The clear, slow-moving water makes fly selection very important. Be sure to come with a varied selection because what slayed them yesterday sometimes falls flat tomorrow.

A weir dam is located about a mile downstream of Norris Dam and provides aeration and controls the fall of water downstream. This weir dam creates a large, slow pool that is full of large trout. Dry-fly fishing in the weir pool is not very practical as the trout tend to do most of their feeding subsurface. You may occasionally find some consistent risers, but you will generally have the best results with a midge pupa rather than a dry fly. Midges, scuds, and sowbugs are the most common trout foods here. The best method is to fish a small nymph pattern from a strike indicator. Since the current is extremely slow this can feel like bobber fishing in a pond. Pick a nice patch of water and make the same drift over and over. The trout cruise so one will eventually

find your fly if you keep it in a good spot. Action is almost always relatively slow here, but hang on when you do hook one. Large fish are common. If this style of fishing is too slow for you, try stripping a small Woolly Bugger, or head to riffles downstream. Be extremely careful when wading in the weir pool, while it's shallow enough to wade when the generators are off, there are plenty of deep dropoffs. Anyone that wades far into the pool will do so by wading along a maze of rock ledges. Be sure to start wading to shore before the generators come on. Finding your way back in rising water can be tricky and the water rises quickly this close to the turbines.

Mayfly nymphs and caddis larvae are present in good numbers in all other sections of the river, but don't neglect

Would you like to "super size" that? Throw large streamers from a boat for a shot at the Clinch River's trophy browns.

Fishing the Sulphur hatch on a summer afternoon.

Clinch River Tailwater

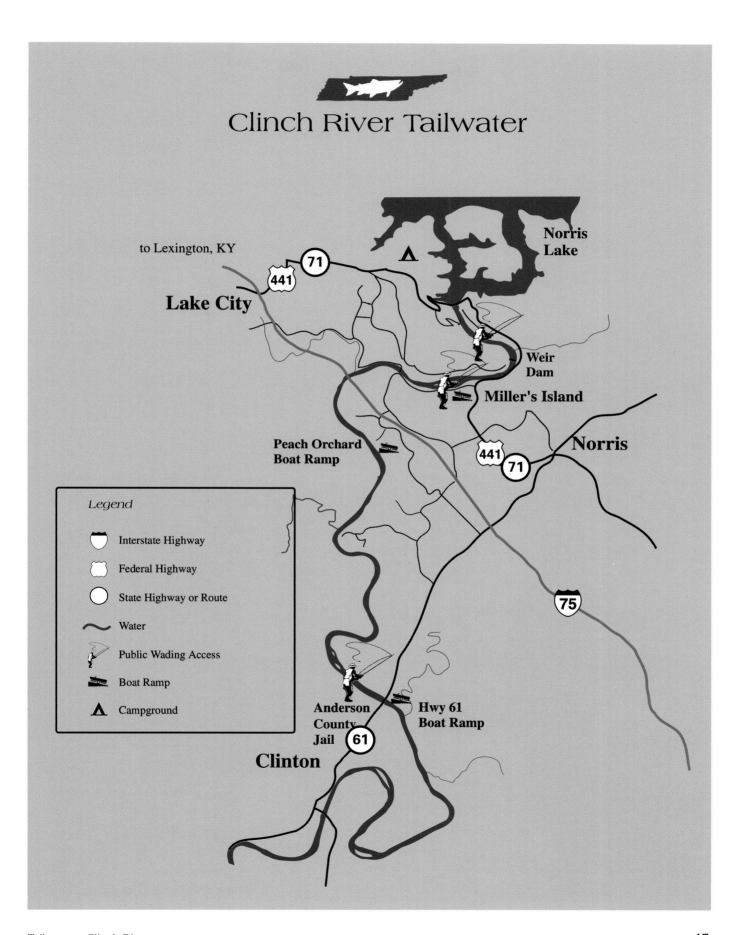

to Lexington, KY

71
441

Lake City

Norris Lake

Weir Dam

Miller's Island

Peach Orchard Boat Ramp

441 **71**

Norris

Legend

- 🛡 Interstate Highway
- 🛡 Federal Highway
- ⚪ State Highway or Route
- 〰 Water
- 🎣 Public Wading Access
- 🚤 Boat Ramp
- ⛺ Campground

75

Anderson County Jail

Hwy 61 Boat Ramp

61

Clinton

the midges. Steadily rising fish can be good dry-fly targets, particularly when sulphurs are hatching. However, Clinch River trout seem to have a weakness for emergers so don't press the issue if you can't get a take with a dry fly. Unweighted Pheasant Tail Nymphs can be very effective when fished to risers during the Sulphur hatch. Soft hackles should also find a place in your fly box during caddis emergences.

Wading

Wading options are somewhat limited on the Clinch unless you have a friend with private access. There are really only a few options. The area with the most access is just below Norris Dam. The river above the weir dam can be difficult to wade because of shallow ledges that suddenly drop into deeper water. Several fishermen prefer to fish this area with a belly boat to eliminate the risk of falling off the ledges. Be sure to head for the bank before the generators are scheduled to come on. The river is accessible below the weir dam but there are limited places to park a car.

The popular Miller's Island access and boat launch provides a good entry to the river a short distance from the dam. There is an abundance of riffles and runs here which are often kinder to fishermen than the flat water above the weir. There is intermittent access downstream of Miller's Island down to Massengill Bridge. This water is generally flat with a few shoals. The water rises and falls in about twenty to thirty minutes since the dam is not too far away.

The next easy access for the wader is at the Anderson County Detention Center in Clinton off Highway 61. In addition to keeping track of generation schedules, it is important not to get too close to the prison or you'll set off a bevy of alarms that will be sure to delay your trip to the river. This section of river has the most shoals for the wader that enjoys fishing water with some flow. The Highway 61 boat ramp, across the river from the jail, affords some access for the wader, but the water gets too deep very quickly. The water usually rises here about four or five hours after the turbines come on depending on the amount of generation. It takes about seven hours for the water to fall after the turbines turn off.

Even a period of only a few hours of zero generation can provide a full day of fishing. Start by fishing while the generators are off near the dam. When the water rises, leave to fish at Clinton. Sometimes by the time the water rises at Clinton, the generators have turned off and the water is low at the dam again.

The Clinch is easily accessible from Interstate 75. Getting off at the Norris exit puts you squarely between the dam and the lower section near the jail. Turning south on highway 61 will take you to Clinton. Turn right immediately after crossing the river over the bridge to park at the prison. To get on the upper river near the dam turn north on Highway 61. After

Hooked up during the Sulphur hatch.

passing the Museum of Appalachia look for the left turn to Norris Dam. You will pass the Miller's Island access and boat ramp on the way to the dam.

Floating

The Clinch is one of the easier tailwaters to float. There aren't any dangerous spots when the water is at a good level to float, one or no generators. The biggest threat is bottoming out on shallow riffles and ledges. The river is fishable with one generator but should be considered not wadeable. Fishing a sulphur hatch with one generator can be excellent. These are also good conditions to fish streamers.

Drift boats, rafts, and john boats are the best craft to employ if the river is generating. Canoes will work best when flow is minimal. Anyone floating in a john boat needs to use caution. There are several places that could easily separate your outboard engine from the transom if approached incorrectly.

Floating the Clinch can also pair well with wading. You may consider floating into a shoal and wading until the water comes up. Floating the river in a canoe or other small craft is an excellent way to gain access to productive shoals that are otherwise off limits. However, this requires a period of no generation. Once the water rises, you can ride the current to your take-out. Some also prefer to use canoes or personal pontoon watercraft to fish the weir pool. This takes away the risk out of filling your waders from a wrong step. There is a canoe access on the weir pool. This should only be used when the generators are off. Do not, under any circumstances, try to float over the weir dam.

A full-day float may start at the Miller's Island launch and end at the Peach Orchard ramp. However, take note that much of the water from Massengill Bridge to the Peach Orchard boat ramp is deep and slow. The most popular float is from the Peach Orchard ramp to the ramp at Highway 61. Peach Orchard is also the best spot to launch if you plan on doing any wade fishing during periods of no power generation.

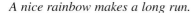

A nice rainbow makes a long run.

A typical Clinch River brown trout.

Floating from Miller's Island to Peach Orchard is relatively short and is impractical when the water is not running. If there is no generation you'll either be dragging the boat over shallow riffles or rowing through still spots. Look for one generator for this float. Float with two generators and you'll make it to Peach Orchard in only a short amount of time. These are pretty tough conditions to catch trout.

One method of floating that can be productive is to put in just before the water rises. The fish usually become a bit more active when the water rises. Action can be excellent if you can manage to stay with the crest of rising water. You may want to anchor along a pod of nice fish but you'll end up behind the rising water. It may be worth it, though.

The river is safe to float in a raft, drift boat, or john boat when two generators are pushing water, although it's not favorable. The best way to characterize a fishing trip with two generators is a fast boat ride. Do not expect to find any rising fish. Also, currents will generally be too deep and swift to make nymph fishing practical. This is the time to throw big, oversized streamers on a sinking line or use hardware on a spinning outfit. Fish will often rise when one generator is running water on the Clinch. Fish that aren't rising will also take nymphs presented blindly in good feeding lanes. However, this is also a good time to consider casting streamers if action on dry flies and nymphs is slow. This is also the best method to hook up with one of the rare stripers in the river. Flies that push a lot of water and have lots of action work best. Be sure to work all logjams and eddies along the bank. A larger rod such as a seven-weight will make the chore of casting a big fly easier and chances are good that the fish will equal the rod.

Alternatives

The Clinch is a little over an hour from other trout water in the area. If generation schedules keep you out of the water, check to see what is happening on the Holston River; it's is a little over an hour away. Also, Little River and Great Smoky Mountains National Park are approximately 90 minutes away.

Tailwaters
Duck River

While the Duck River is not Tennessee's most popular trout fishing destination it is worthy of mention. It's only a short distance from the Elk River tailwater below Tims Ford Dam and there are a number of similarities between the two rivers. Both are the only quality trout waters in south-central Tennessee. Both are in rolling farm country that features corn, cotton, cattle, and Tennessee walking horses.

Perhaps the most uncanny similarity is that both have famous distilleries nearby. Jack Daniels is in Lynchburg, just minutes from the Elk and George Dickel is in Normandy, only a stone's throw from the Duck River.

Most Duck River fishermen seem to prefer the Elk, and rely on the Duck as a backup. The river is fairly small which can make it easy for wading if water conditions are right.

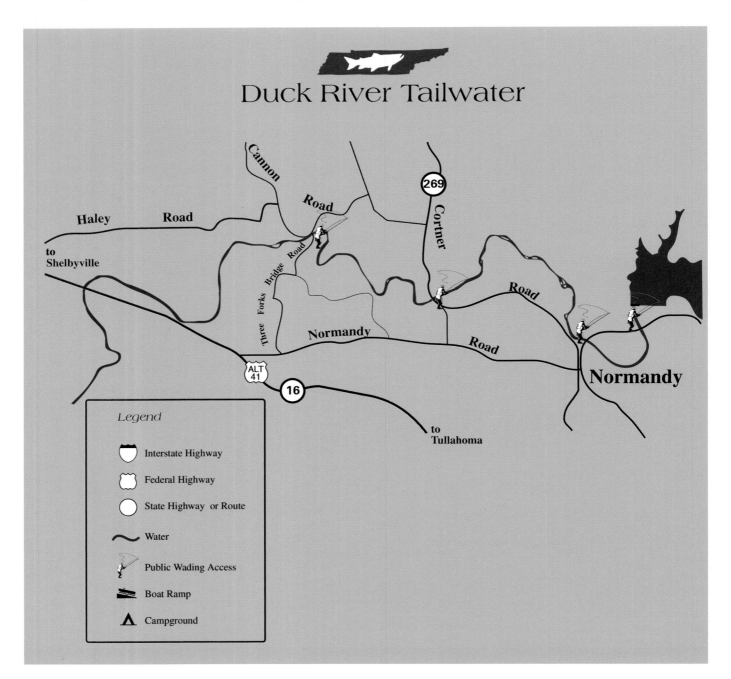

Look for flows of 200 cfs or less. The river is a bit too small for boats typically used for floating trout rivers. Canoes are a common sight and are probably the best suited craft to float down the river. Personal pontoon craft are also a means of fishing more secluded runs on the Duck.

While the Duck offers plenty of trout for the fishermen, very few will ever grow to be very large. Browns and rainbows are both caught. Flashy streamer patterns are among the most successful, but soft hackles should find a place in your fly box. Casting them down and across easy runs can hook a good number of fish. Beadhead nymphs work just as well here as they do everywhere else.

Shelbyville is the closest sizeable town to the Duck River, but Tullahoma isn't far in the opposite direction. There is plenty of food and lodging in either of these towns. Neither of these towns have direct access to an interstate but I-24 is the closest. You should consult a road map to find the best route from your location.

Wading

There are several public access points on the river. The most popular is the river access directly below the dam. The spot can be crowded though, so you might consider one of several other spots. There is a nearby parking area adjacent to the bridge on Normandy Road just before you reach the dam. This is private property but the landowner is currently allowing fishermen to cross his land. There is a sign that requests that you keep the area clean. Please respect this request.

The next access point as you go downstream is at a bridge that crosses Cortner Road. There is a gravel lot here and you can drive down to the river bank to drop or retrieve a canoe. The best water is immediately downstream. There is also river access at Three Fork Bridge. None of these parking areas has restrooms so use one before you get to the river.

Floating

Fishing the Duck from a small craft may be a bit cramped if you choose to remain in your canoe. Staying far enough back from your target may not give you enough casting room on the backside. The best method on the Duck is to use your canoe or personal pontoon as a freighter to transport you between places to wade on good runs of water.

Alternatives

The Elk River is the only other trout river that can be reached quickly if conditions change unexpectedly. Check generation schedules on the Caney Fork, too, but the drive might push two hours if leaving from Normandy.

Duck River brown.

Elk River

The Elk River is among the least known of Tenessee's tailwaters. While its waters may be somewhat obscure to many fishermen, an internationally known Tennesee trademark is produced only a short distance down the road. The Jack Daniels distillery was built on the sight of a spring near Lynchburg because of the superior qualities it lent to the whiskey. Waters in this region are agreeable to trout as well as bourbon. The Elk's relative seclusion from most other trout fisheries accounts for its anonymity. The Duck River is the only other consistent trout fishery in the vicinity.

The river is easily wadeable when water flow is prime for fishing. Most of the river is less than thigh deep with few places exceeding chest deep. Look for a flow of under 100 cubic feet per second for these conditions. However, the river is fishable up to about 300 cfs. This information available on the TVA river flow hotline or at TVA's rivers and environment web site, http://lakeinfo.tva.gov/.

The Elk has a look that is somewhat distinctive from other tailwaters in Tennessee. Most of the other trout water in the state is in or around mountains. The Elk winds among lazily rolling hills and takes a slow pace. The river flows through cow pastures, corn rows, and woods. Fishermen are likely to catch fish other than rainbow and brown trout. Smallmouth bass are always a possibility, in addition to a variety of sunfishes.

Virtually all of the trout in the river have a hatchery in their past. Most fish will be between 9 and 14 inches. Some fish will carry over though, so larger trout are a possibility. While rainbows and browns seem to do well once they are in the river, conditions are not favorable for spawning. The river bottom doesn't have the proper combination of gravel and current for a successful spawn.

Aquatic insects aren't as numerous in the Elk as they are in several of the other tailwaters. While there are populations of caddis, midges, and mayflies, they are outnumbered by scuds and snails. As a result, wet-fly and nymph patterns are far more successful than dry-fly patterns. Most Elk River locals fish wet patterns on a down-and-across swing. Small Woolly Buggers are also pretty hard on the trout. The same technique is used with these streamers but short twitches add to the enticement.

The Elk is almost evenly situated between the two small towns of Winchester and Lynchburg. TN 50 connects the two and crosses the river just below Tims Ford Dam. Coming from Chattanooga, exit I-24 at Monteagle and take Highway 41 to Winchester. From Nashville, take I-24 to Highway 231 near Murfreesboro and follow it to Lynchburg.

Wading

The Elk River supports trout for approximately twenty miles downstream of Tims Ford Dam and wading is the best way to fish the river. While access is somewhat limited, there are several good public access points and they are marked. One of the most popular access points is directly below the dam. There is a paved parking lot here and good river access. The water upstream of the parking lot is a still pool under the dam. There are several nice runs you can walk to going downstream.

Only a short distance away is a TVA access at a gravel lot known as Garner's Ford. Coming from Lynchburg, take a right turn before you reach Tims Ford Dam.

The next point down the river is at the Farris Creek Bridge. There is parking on both sides of the river and canoe access on the east side. The water is best suited for wading on the downstream side of the bridge. There are a lot of aquatic weeds in the river where trout can hide. You may see some wade fishermen pull their automobile right down into the river bed but this is foolish. The river rises swiftly and could swamp a vehicle if the river rises unexpectedly.

The last best place to get on the water is at a place called Old Dam Ford. This is a tough place to reach but it has good access. The best way to find this spot is to look for the river access signs off Highway 64 near the Flint fish hatchery. The water here is not as attractive for wading as it is at points upstream, but there are at least a couple of places worth casting a fly. Shiloh Bridge also has some access but this is beginning to get in water that may be questionable for trout in the warmest months.

Floating

The Elk is an easy float for a canoe or personal pontoon. Larger craft such as drift boats and rafts are just a bit too big for this small river. Dragging them over every shoal will take the romance out of any float trip. This will also ruin the fishing for any wade fishermen you drag your boat past. Any generation makes the river far too swift to be safe or practical for fishing. Canoes should not be used under these conditions.

You can put in at Garner's Ford or the dam and float down to Farris Creek Bridge. Another option is to put in at Farris Creek and paddle down to Old Dam Ford. The first of these options is preferable but all will cover a lot of water. It's tough to get any time to fish when you're trying to get downstream before dark. There are a few canoe rental/shuttles on the Elk which may be able to put you on shorter trips that will allow you to fish every run thoroughly.

Alternatives

Check the Duck River if generation schedules aren't favorable for fishing on the Elk. The two rivers are less than an hour apart and water flows on the Duck are a bit more constant than they are on the Elk.

Fishing the Elk near Tims Ford Dam.

Elk River Tailwater

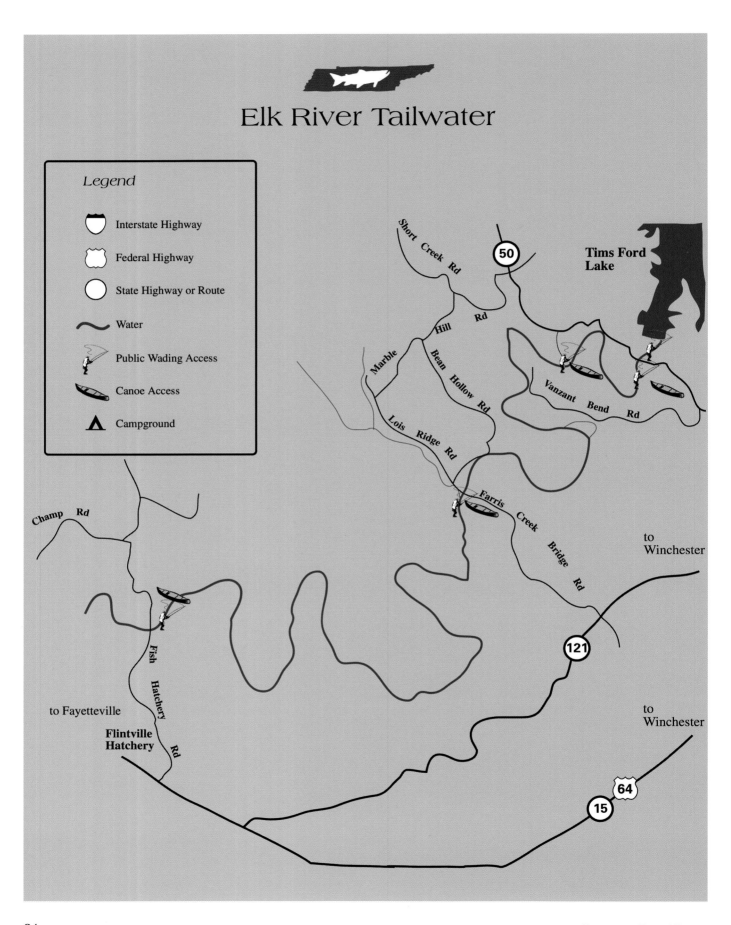

Legend

Interstate Highway
Federal Highway
State Highway or Route
Water
Public Wading Access
Canoe Access
Campground

Short Creek Rd

50

Tims Ford Lake

Hill Rd

Marble

Bean Hollow Rd

Vanzant Bend Rd

Lois Ridge Rd

Farris Creek Bridge Rd

to Winchester

Champ Rd

121

to Winchester

to Fayetteville

Fish Hatchery Rd

Flintville Hatchery

64

15

Tailwaters
Fort Patrick Henry

The Fort Patrick Henry tailwater is a short section of the South Holston River and is remarkably anonymous in spite of the good trout fishing to be found there. It has a relatively short length of water that can be accessed. However, the area that can be accessed is wide open to fishing when there is no generation from the powerhouse.

Patrick Henry falls in the shadow of the South Holston and Watauga tailwaters which are vastly more popular. Both of these rivers have far more water to fish and better generation schedules. Traditionally, Fort Patrick Henry Dam generates in short bursts and remains off for two or three hours in between. A day spent fishing here will be interrupted several times. If you really want to see time fly, fish this short stretch of water when the fish are biting. Two hours can go by in the blink of an eye. Keep a close eye on your watch and a closer eye on the water. Water comes up extremely fast. It's a good idea to get out a few minutes before the generators are scheduled to come on. A few locals spend their lunch hour fishing here.

Fly fishermen typically fish nymph patterns below Fort Patrick Henry. Caddis and midges are the most important aquatic trout foods. There are some hatches of caddis that allow for dry-fly fishing but they are not as reliable as fishing a pupa pattern. Woolly Buggers, as usual, can provide some action if nymph fishing is slow.

Fort Patrick Henry is easily accessible from Interstate 81. Take the exit for Kingsport and Highway 36. Take 36 toward Kingsport and you will drive through the community of Colonial Heights. A bridge crosses the river about two miles from the interstate and access is available on both sides of the bridge.

Wading

There is only one wading access on this tailwater and that is directly below the dam. There is parking on either side of the

Wading below Ft. Patrick Henry.

Water rises several feet in a matter of minutes.

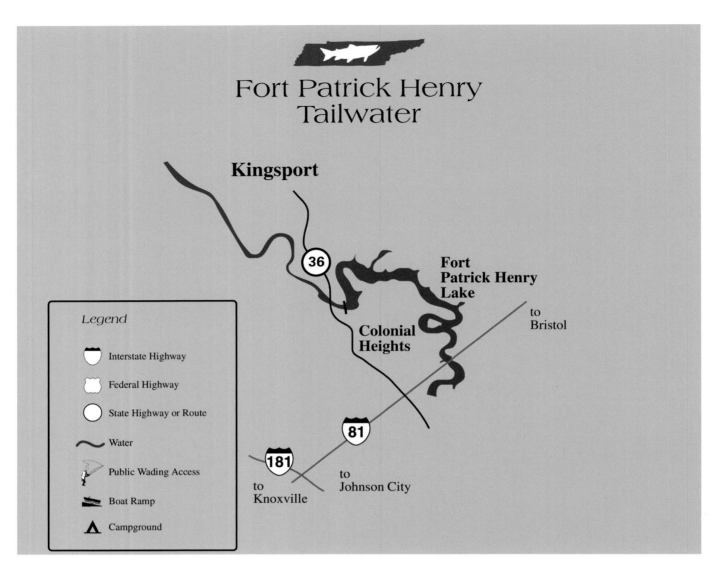

Fort Patrick Henry
Tailwater

Kingsport

36

**Fort
Patrick Henry
Lake**

to
Bristol

**Colonial
Heights**

to
Johnson City

81

181

to
Knoxville

Legend

Interstate Highway

Federal Highway

State Highway or Route

Water

Public Wading Access

Boat Ramp

Campground

river, but the best place to get in is on the south side of the river. If you're coming in from Interstate 81 you'll turn off right before you cross the river. There is a short path from the parking area to the water. Parking and access are available on the other side of the river, but you will have to climb down a steep, rocky bank. That is also the deep side of the river.

The most obvious place to fish is directly under the dam. However, this is pretty slow water and deep enough to make wading a dicey proposition. Walking downstream below the Highway 36 bridge provides river access with some slow runs and much shallower water to wade. There is only a faint path through the woods that follows the river along the south bank. At least a half mile or so of river can be fished this way.

Floating
There are no ramps on this short stretch of trout water.

Alternatives
Fort Patrick Henry is fortunate to be close to the South Holston and Watauga tailwaters. In fact, those rivers are good enough

that most anglers choose those rivers first and consider Patrick Henry as a fallback for times when those waters have less than optimal conditions.

Look for deep slots to drift nymphs.

Tailwaters

Hiwassee River

The Hiwasse is arguably Tennessee's most scenic tailwater. A good portion of it runs through the Cherokee National Forest where there is absoulutely no development beyond the road and an occasional picnic table. In fact, the designated quality zone, often referred to as the "Trophy Section," is only accessible by floating or hiking in. Outside of the forest the Hiwassee meanders through rolling farms with a mountainous back drop. While its trophy opportunities may not be as prolific as other Tennessee tailwaters, many consider it to be their favorite tailwater. The river and its trout have features similar to a giant freestone mountain stream. Trout often rise freely to such attractor patterns as Stimulators and Royal Wulffs. The Hiwassee's extremely wide river bed, over 200 yards in places, can also give a distinctly Western feel to a day's fishing. Long shoals are interspersed with long pools. Islands frequently divide the flow. Catch several trout on a Turck's Tarantula while drift boats

The Hiwassee near Reliance.

float past and you might start to look for the Absaroka or Teton ranges in the distance.

The tailwater begins at the powerhouse below Apalachia Dam. The dam is almost twelve miles upstream of the powerhouse. Water travels through large pipes from the dam to the powerhouse. There is water in the river bed between the dam and powerhouse but its flow is minimal. Freestone tributaries like Coker Creek flow into the pre-TVA river bed and maintain some flow. There are some trout in the lower sections above the powerhouse during the cooler months but it is primarily a smallmouth bass fishery, and a good one at that.

The Hiwassee can be full of recreational boaters and tubers on weekends from Memorial Day through Labor Day. There will almost always be a few on the river any day of the week, but weekends are the worst. Most of these funyaks and tubes will be found from the powerhouse boat ramp down to Reliance where most of the boats were rented. Many of these floaters take to the river late in the morning or early in the afternoon. Your best bet to dodge them would be to hit the river early and late.

There are very few tubers downstream of Reliance. However, wading access declines with them. While the river is still wadeable below Reliance, it is more suited to the float fisher. Much of the best water is beyond roadside access. There are still public access points at Forest Service picnic areas, however. There is also a state park near the confluence of Gee Creek on the north side of the river. Camping and a boat ramp are also available here.

Trout are still present in the river downstream of Highway 411 but this is not really a section of river that should be considered by the casual, wading fisherman. A boat is needed, but the water is not at all fierce and john boats are a common sight. Smallmouth bass are at least as common as trout and may be an incidental catch if streamers or large nymphs are your fly of choice. This part of the river fishes best in the spring and late winter. Water temperatures are generally too high later in the season to make this a desirable trout fishing destination. Putting a boat in at Highway 411 requires a full-day float to the take-out at Patty Bridge.

As with all trout fishing in Tennessee, spring is the best time to fish the Hiwassee. Hatches are usually at their best in April and continue well into June. Insect populations in the Hiwassee are almost as diverse as they are in mountain streams. This is probably a result of the Hiwassee's several tributaries. The Hiwassee's caddis hatches may be the best of any river in the region. I recall one spring evening when trout made slashing rises to caddis that hatched in numbers that gave the appearance of snow. In addition to caddis, look for mayflies. Hendricksons, blue-winged olives, Quill Gordons, and *Isonychias* all make seasonal appearances.

Mid summer can be good but conditions tend to vary year to year. Hot, dry years take their toll on this tailwater.

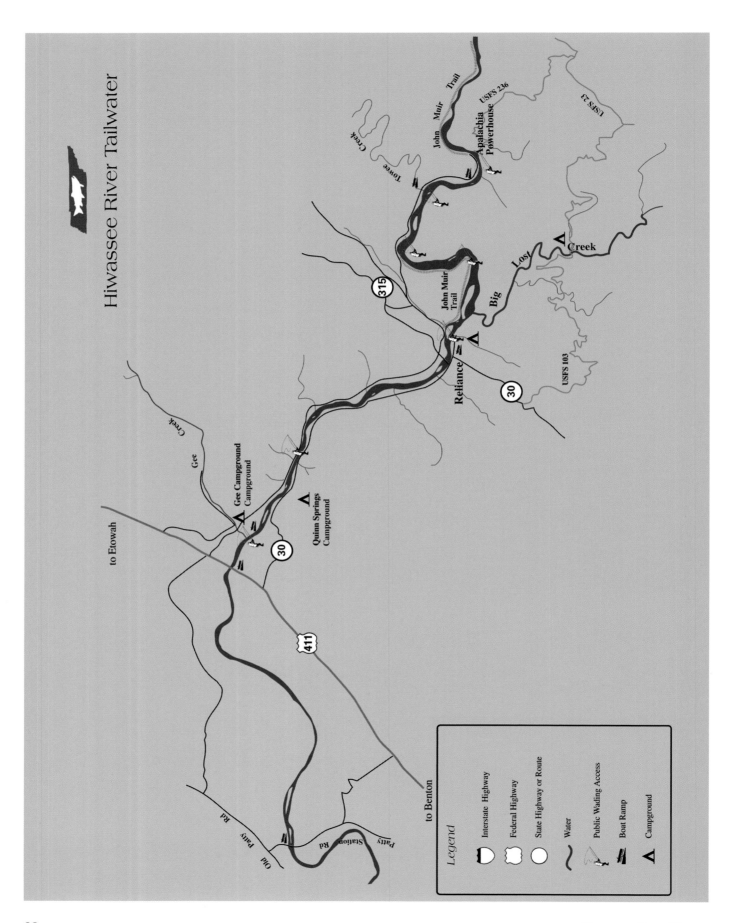

Hiwassee River Tailwater

John Muir Trail

USFS 236

USFS 23

Towee Creek

Apalachia Powerhouse

315

John Muir Trail

Big Lost Creek

Reliance

30

USFS 103

Gee Creek

to Etowah

Gee Campground Campground

Quinn Springs Campground

30

411

to Benton

Old Patty Rd

Patty Station Rd

Legend

	Interstate Highway
	Federal Highway
	State Highway or Route
	Water
	Public Wading Access
	Boat Ramp
	Campground

Apalachia reservoir which feeds the river is a relatively shallow lake. If sufficient rain does not fall through the spring and summer, lake levels can become dangerously low. Lake levels need to be deep to maintain cold temperatures on the bottom where the water is drawn into the tailwater. Even during a good year, water temperatures are comfortable for the fisherman who has forgotten his waders. In fact, many prefer wet wading in July and August. *Isonychias* continue to hatch most evenings and Sulphurs and blue-winged olives can also be present. Big attractor dry flies are the most popular with fishers, though. Turck's Tarantula, Stimulators, Chernobyl Ants, Madame X's, and large hopper patterns all bring trout to the surface. They seem to be most effective along ledges, banks, or the edges of grass.

Autumn is usually a season of slow fishing on the Hiwassee. TVA usually begins its draw-down of reservoirs shortly after Labor Day so generation schedules are not very kind to the wading fisherman. Seasonal turnover of Apalachia Lake also means warmer water temperatures which does little to stimulate the fishing. It's ironic since the time when the weather cools, the water warms up.

Winter fishing can be good enough to justify a visit. While dry-fly fishing may not be anywhere near its peak, trout can easily be caught on nymphs and streamers. Small winter stoneflies are among the most common insects to hatch, peaking in late winter. Trout can often be found rising in calmer waters. Most will be feeding on midges or small olives.

Wading

The Hiwassee River is among the best tailwaters for the wading fisherman. Since there is excellent public access inside the Cherokee National Forest, many fishermen can be dispersed over a large area. Other tailwater fisheries aren't as kind, packing most of the wading fishermen into a relatively small portion of the river. All of the best spots to wade are upstream of Highway 411. The Quinn Springs picnic area is the most developed of several roadside pull-outs between 411 and Reliance. Access can also be had at the Webb Store in Reliance. Crossing the bridge at Reliance, and taking every possible right turn, will take you to the upper section of the tailwater. You will pass the Childers Creek access along this route which is inside the trophy section. Coming over the crest of Hood Mountain you will have an excellent view of the river. The "Stair Steps" are visible to the right. Once the road rejoins the river at the Big Bend parking area there is continuous roadside access all

Wading the upper part of the Trophy Section when only one generator is operating.

the way to Apalachia Powerhouse. This is the favorite stretch of river for waders. Some fishermen hike the John Muir Trail which follows the river from the Big Bend parking area on the upstream end to the Childers Creek parking area on the downstream end. This is three miles of river that receives little pressure from wading fishermen. You might also consider this area for a walk-in or float-in camping trip.

The entire river from the powerhouse downstream to the Big Bend parking area has excellent access for the wader. Furthermore, this is probably the only tailwater where waders often prefer some water flowing from the turbines. In fact, this is the only tailwater that has wading possibilities, albeit with caution, when two generators are operating.

Waders need to be aware of generation schedules. A good deal of the river is accessible with one generator or none. The most experienced fishermen on the Hiwassee prefer to wade the river with a "pulsing" schedule. This is usually about three hours of no generation followed by one hour of generation. This schedule is common in the spring when water is being held back to fill Apalachia Lake. Water levels will rise with the one generator but it is generally mild. However, those spots that are only marginal to wade will become too rough. Just be aware of when the water will rise so you don't end up stranded on the wrong side of the river. (Maybe you should take note of the time so you can get stranded, having no choice but to fish until the water recedes.) The water generally takes about two hours to reach Reliance from the powerhouse. That leaves plenty of time to pack up when the generators kick on and run downstream for a few more hours of fishing.

Some areas are wadeable with two generators, but these can take some experience to find. One of the easiest spots to fish with two generators is just downstream of the powerhouse. Cross the suspension bridge over the river to get to the other side. At least one third of the river bed is wadeable for several hundred yards downstream of the bridge. Several spots in the trophy section are also wadeable for the experienced wader. The best way to become familiar with these spots is to either have someone show you or float the river with two generators, taking note of shallow spots.

The Hiwassee is set back some distance from Interstate 75 but is easily accessible from US 411. You can exit I-75 at Athens and take TN 39 to Etowah and 411. The Hiwassee is about ten minutes south of Etowah. Coming from the south it will be more convenient to exit onto TN 311 and take the Highway 64 and 74 bypass along the edge of Cleveland. Follow Highway 64 and 74 to 411. Take 411 north through Benton to the Hiwassee. The river is about ten minutes from Benton.

Floating

A boat launch is situated about a quarter mile downstream of the powerhouse. This is a good place to launch for either a full or half-day float. A leisurely half-day float would terminate at the Towee Creek ramp and picnic area.

The best generation schedule for the float fisherman is two generators. Much of the upper river is floatable with only one generator but you will drag bottom several times. The best section of the upper river to float is from the boat launch near the powerhouse down to the Towee Creek access. The shoals are deep enough here to make it with just one generator. Be sure you know what Towee Creek looks like from the river or you might float past and have to take-out at Reliance. This is generally a half-day float or a full day with long stops.

Even a full-day float launched from the powerhouse ramp will have many long stops before taking out at Reliance. A non-stop float can be done in about two and a half hours when two generators are pushing water. If you have a full day to float the river, take your time and fish all the fishy-looking spots.

Doug Sanders with a nice Hiwassee brown.

The quality zone is an excellent section to float. Boats will launch at the powerhouse for a long float, or launch at Towee Creek for a more targeted float through the Trophy Section. Many of the best trout caught every year come from this secluded stretch of big water. The best-known piece of water here would be the Stair Steps. This set of ledges drops about eight feet over a few hundred yards. While it is not an overly dangerous piece of water to float, an inexperienced boater could easily hang up or worse. Get some local advice before taking a drift boat or large raft through the Stair Steps. Devil's Shoal sounds worse than it is. While caution should be exercised, take comfort in the fact that countless weekend fun-seekers have floated through in inflatable funyaks.

Launching at Reliance and floating down to the boat ramp at Highway 411 can be a good float that shouldn't be crowded. However, remember that crowds tend to flock to the best spots. Once again this can be a relatively short trip so there's no point rushing past rising trout. This stretch of water can be very difficult to maneuver if the water is low since there is an abundance of shallow shoals. This is probably the least-floated section of the river since most fishermen prefer the upper part of the river when conditions are good, and are forced to float a lower section when the water is low. There is also a ramp on the north side of the river, at Gee Creek campground just upstream of Highway 411.

The only realistic floating option when there is little to no water generation is to put in at Highway 411 and drift downstream. This section lacks the shoals so common in the upper river, so a change of twelve inches in depth means little with regard to navigating a boat.

Small personal pontoon water craft are ideal for the Hiwassee. Since there is so much roadside access, it is easy to put-in and take-out almost anywhere you please. It was from my inflatable pontoon craft that I learned several wading spots in high water. However, the boat was required just to reach several of them. A canoe may be used to freighter from one wadeable spot to another but only for experienced paddlers. The abundance of swift water and rocks might capsize inexperienced paddlers.

You may see some fishermen fishing deep holes from belly boats. This is an acceptable method for fishing deep holes during periods of no generation. However, a belly boat should not be used under any circumstances to float the river. The Hiwassee has too many spots that are far too treacherous for a belly boat. In fact, there have been several drownings and a few more close calls involving belly boats.

Be aware of the quality-zone regulations if you plan on keeping some trout during a long float from the upper river down to Reliance. All trout you keep must comply with the regulations, regardless of whether it was caught in the quality zone or upstream from it. That goes for your tackle as well. Personal floatation devices must also be worn while floating the river, regardless of the craft you're in.

Alternatives

Most fishermen might want to look for an alternate place to fish if two generators are running constantly and a boat can't be secured. None of the other tailwaters are convenient to the Hiwassee if conditions are poor. However, there are a number of freestone alternatives if you need to find someplace else. Gee Creek is a small tributary that flows into the river just upstream of Highway 411. This small freestone stream can be accessed via a trail that goes into the Gee Creek Wilderness. Big Lost Creek is also another good spot to try that is not too far. A Forest Service campground is also available here and it is generally quieter than those on the river. The Tellico River and its elaborate tributary system are about an hour away.

Drift boats are a common sight on the Hiwassee.

Tailwaters
Holston River

The Holston River tailwater below Cherokee Dam is the newest trout-fishing destination in Tennessee. TWRA began stocking trout in the river in the mid 1990s on an experimental basis. Most expected the Holston to be a strictly put-and-take fishery. However, water temperatures remain favorable for trout year round and the river has quickly become a quality fishery. The Holston winds through rolling hills and green pastures, and eventually flows on to join the French Broad to form the Tennessee River.

The Holston fishes like a typical tailwater. Midges are among the top food items that the trout eat. Small nymphs provide the bulk of the action for the fly fisherman. There is a decent caddis population, though, and this can make for some excellent dry-fly fishing. Blue-winged Olives are also present, but hatch less reliably than the midges and caddis. Midges are a year-round affair, while the best caddis hatches occur during the warmer months. The best caddis patterns are light colored and about a size 18. Emerger patterns are often more effective than dry flies. Terrestrial patterns also turn some heads during the summer. The agricultural country around the Holston produces good numbers of hoppers and Japanese beetles.

The river is easily accessible from Jefferson City coming off Interstate 40. You can take TN 40 all the way from I-40 to the dam. Some fishermen coming from Knoxville may prefer to take Highway 11E, locally known as Andrew Johnson Highway. However, access to the lower end of the river may be gained quicker via 11W, locally called Rutledge Pike, if you're coming from Knoxville.

Finding your way around the Holston can be a bit confusing. Many of the roads that follow the river or lead to an access are extremely narrow and seem to go in circles. Locals who grew up on these roads travel at high speed, so be sure to hug your side of the road on blind curves.

Wading
While the fishing on the Holston is excellent, access is only fair. The boat ramps are the only areas for public access. This limits

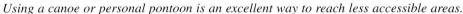

Using a canoe or personal pontoon is an excellent way to reach less accessible areas.

Holston River Tailwater

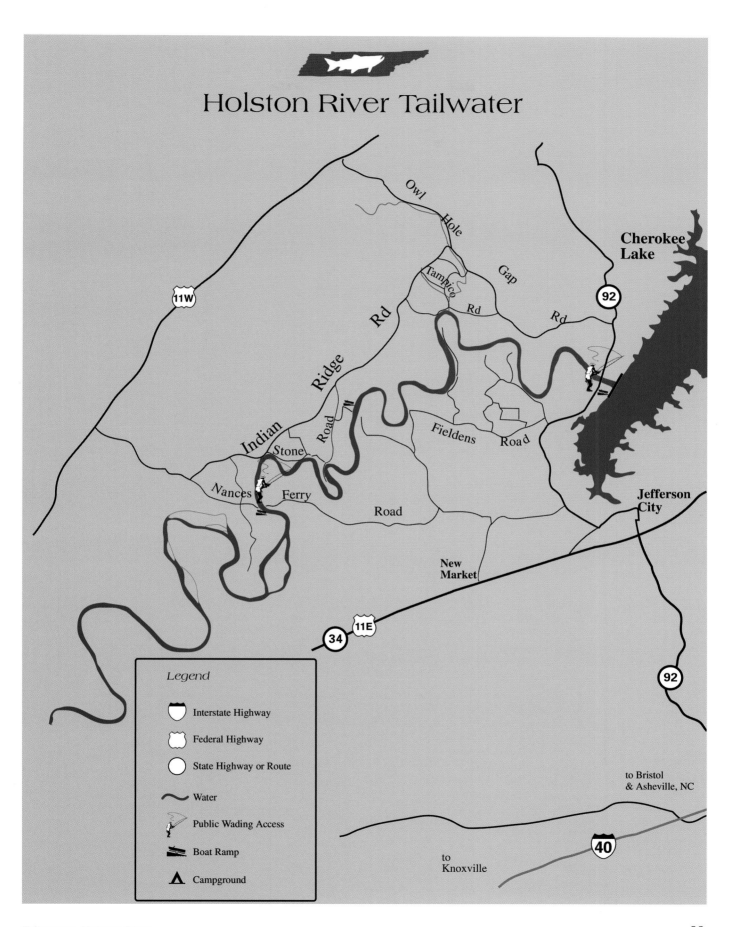

Legend

- Interstate Highway
- Federal Highway
- State Highway or Route
- Water
- Public Wading Access
- Boat Ramp
- Campground

Trout are flourishing in the Holston.

opportunities for the wading fisherman. The Nance's Ferry ramp has the best water from winter through early summer. Water temperatures will warm and become marginal later in the year. Smallmouth bass are prolific throughout the river but may be your only catch in this section during the summer and fall.

Access is also possible at the boat ramp near Cherokee Dam. However, the water right here is too deep to wade. Walking downstream can put you in better water. There are shoals about a half mile downstream of the ramp and usually fish well for those who are willing to walk.

There is another spot for waders to keep in mind. It is barely more than a wide spot in the road downstream of where Buffalo Springs flows into the Holston. It is likely on private property but has been used by fishermen for years. Be sure to keep things clean here so this spot will not become posted in the future. This spot is not practical for launching or pulling boats out of the water. The river bank is steep so only anglers with a strong back should consider bringing a canoe up or down the bank; pontoon craft would be much easier.

If you plan to wade, look for periods of no generation or days when generation comes in short pulses. You will probably need to evacuate the river during a pulse, particularly in the upper stretches closest to the dam. These pulses make the river easier to float, though. Otherwise, things can get pretty shallow.

Water temperatures can be comfortable for wading during the warmest months. Fishermen might consider shedding their waders on the hottest days and bare-leg it. While the water isn't too cold in the summer, you will probably stay warmer on a rainy day if you use your waders.

Floating

Those who float the river will find far more opportunities. However, if you plan to float you'll need to launch early at the dam if you expect to get to the ramp at Indian Cave at a decent hour. When water flows are ideal for fishing, this float is really too long to be practical. Another option is to put in at Indian Cave and float to Nance's Ferry. Again, this is a long float so be sure to allow for plenty of time. While drift boats and fishing rafts are ideal for use on the Holston, many fishermen may get more service from a canoe or personal pontoon craft. These are far easier to launch or pull from roadside areas that don't have a ramp. Most of the river is relatively easy-going with relatively mild shoals. In fact, if you're rowing a drift boat or raft it may be too easy-going in some spots. There can be long stretches of flat water that will exhaust an oarsman.

Alternatives

The Holston River is a little way from other trout fisheries but someone willing to drive an hour or a few minutes more can reach alternate spots if need be. The Clinch is a little over an hour away. The tailwater below Fort Patrick Henry is also a little over an hour up Interstate 81. However, anyone driving as far as Patrick Henry might just invest a few more minutes to get to the South Holston or Watauga.

There are also a few freestoners you might consider; the Middle Prong of the Pigeon River and its tributaries are probably the closest, with Cosby Creek coming in a close second. Buffalo Spring Creek isn't really a freestone but it does have trout and is a direct tributary of the Holston. It is stocked regularly but access is generally limited to a few hundred yards which are usually packed with local fishermen.

The Holston at sunset.

The Holston is a large tailwater river.

The Obey River is a short tailwater below Dale Hollow Dam which is maintained by the US Army Corps of Engineers. While the length of water that may be fished is relatively short, this is big water. While it is wadeable when the generators are off, a small boat will open more opportunities. The stretch of water is short because the Obey merges with the Cumberland River only six miles from Dale Hollow Dam.

The bulk of the trout caught from the Obey will be straight from the stocking truck. However, any trout that can manage to hold over will grow. Rainbows and browns are both stocked regularly but the Obey holds an odd distinction in Tennessee trout fishing. The state-record cutthroat trout came from the Obey River in 1969. It's weight of 6 ounces isn't particularly impressive, though. The fish was probably one of several stocked in the river that year but cutthroats are no longer stocked by TWRA.

The Obey's proximity to the Cumberland has a direct effect on the rate at which water falls when the generators turn off. Water will fall somewhat rapidly if the Cumberland is low. However, it can take a while to drop off if the Cumberland River is running high.

Many of the trout in the Obey are fresh stockers and will respond to a number of fly patterns. However, holdovers begin to develop an eye for midges. Small midge larvae and pupae patterns are often the best patterns to fool the best trout.

Wading

Even though there is not as much mileage on this river as most others, there is a decent amount of access to the tailwater. The uppermost wading access is just below Dale Hollow Dam at an Army Corps of Engineers recreational day-use area. Going down the river, the next one is known as Moody's Bend. This is really a fishing pier as much as a wading access point. The third access is in Celina at Donaldson Park.

Floating

The Obey is easily floatable in a variety of craft as long as water isn't flowing from Dale Hollow Dam. There are boat ramps at every public access so it is quite easy to float most of the tailwater in one outing.

Alternatives

The Obey stands as a lone trout fishery in north-central Tennessee. However, it is not far from the Cumberland River tailwater in south-central Kentucky. In fact, most fishermen driving in the direction of the Obey are only doing so in order to get to the Cumberland. Generation schedules for the Cumberland can be obtained from TVA and checking Wolf Creek Dam, number 34 on the menu.

The Caney Fork is the only other trout fishery within a reasonable distance of the Obey. It's at least an hour's drive away.

Typical Obey River rainbow trout.

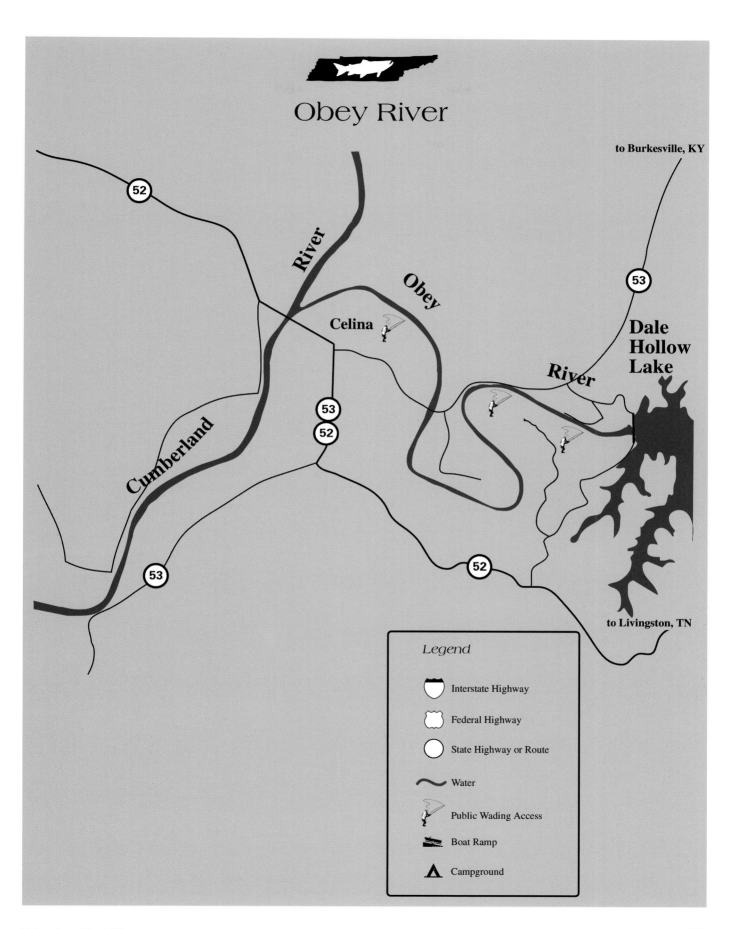

Obey River

to Burkesville, KY

52

53

River

Obey

Celina

Cumberland

River

Dale Hollow Lake

53

52

53

52

to Livingston, TN

Legend

Interstate Highway

Federal Highway

State Highway or Route

Water

Public Wading Access

Boat Ramp

Campground

Tailwaters
South Holston River

Over the years, the South Holston has quietly assumed the rank of top tailwater in Tennessee if not the entire eastern United States. The South Fork of the Holston flows south from the Virginia mountains into South Holston Lake. From this lake it emerges as the South Holston tailwater. Locals generally refer to the tailwater as the South Holston and the river above the lake as the South Fork of the Holston. This pastoral tailwater hosts excellent insect hatches throughout the year. Large trout can be found rising to mayflies during the best hatches. The river bottom is quite literally crawling with aquatic insects. Trout populations are high in the South Holston, and wild fish have good conditions to spawn. The fish do not come easy, though. These trout can be as picky as those in any spring creek. In fact, it is most commonly described as a spring creek. One frustrated fly-fisher once told me after a long day he was ready to count refusals as trout caught and released.

The South Holston is renowned for its brown trout.

Food is so plentiful in the South Holston that many trout hesitate to move very far to eat. A light presentation coupled with a perfect drift is what it takes. Don't forget the fly, though. This river is a fly technician's paradise. Effective flies include some sort of emerger, stillborn, or cripple imitation. In spite of this, the South Holston may be any fly-fisher's best shot at a large trout on a dry fly.

The fish are most difficult during low flows when the water is clear and shallow. Current is minimal. The trout have a better attitude when a hatch is in progress during power generation. This is generally for boaters only, though. The South Holston has been jokingly referred to as a damp parking lot when there is no flow from the dam. Pushes and wakes will often reveal trout cruising across shallow slicks.

Access is relatively good for the wading angler. In fact, this river usually has flows that are negotiable for both boaters and waders. While wading is not practical during power generation, you may be able to fish the upper stretches of the river early in the day and run downstream when the water rises to get in several more hours of fishing.

Sulphurs, blue-winged olives, midges, and black caddis are the most predominant hatches. Sowbug imitations also produce, particularly on days when there is little surface activity. The height of the Sulphur hatch takes place in June and continues through the summer. However, Sulphurs might appear any day of the year. I've fished the river on snowy days in January and seen Sulphurs struggle to get off the water. Blue-winged olives are also extremely common. While they may appear at any time, they tend to hatch best in the worst weather. Dreary, rainy or snowy days might have thick emergences of size 18-20 olives.

The labyrinth weir dam dramatically increases dissolved oxygen and slows the fall of water.

Always keep midge patterns on hand. The fish will often switch over to midges when a hatch of Sulphurs or olives begins to peter out. Sometimes midges will be the only hatch of the day. These are often the most maddening days on the river. You can often see fish feeding only a few feet away and be lucky to fool a only few.

Large rainbows and browns are often caught during heavy hatches. However, the best way to hook a nice brown might be to streamer-fish from a boat during generation. This will generally be slower fishing than anchoring off a pod of risers, but the average fish will often be larger. Shad minnows are often sucked through the turbines in the fall and this is a prime time to employ this tactic. A light-colored streamer with some flash just might fool the trout of a lifetime.

Just like anywhere else, the South Holston has the most activity in the spring and early summer. However, this river fishes extremely well all year long. I've often looked forward to snowy winter days on the South Holston. Only hard-core fishermen are on the river, and there is a decent opportunity for good dry-fly fishing. Action will pick up with the crowds as the weather warms.

The South Holston is somewhat different from other Tennessee tailwaters because it has a good population of wild trout. There are several areas where trout are able to spawn successfully. As a result, action has been taken to protect spawning trout and the eggs they lay. Not all of the river has suitable spawning habitat and large numbers of fish tend to congregate on a few shoals with necessary gravel. A coalition of local anglers were concerned that large spawners packed into a few tight spots might tempt unethical fishermen to try snagging. Another issue was that any fishermen wading these areas could damage the redds and inflict a high mortality rate on the eggs. Two stretches of the river now have seasonal closures to protect spawning fish and the South Holston's wild fish.

While a few other rivers have quality zones the South Holston has regulations that protect larger fish throughout its length. Currently it's illegal to possess any trout 16 -22 inches. Only one trout over 22 inches may be kept, while up to seven fish under 16 inches can be creeled. This regulation protects the bulk of mature trout that will spawn.

Getting to the South Holston is not that difficult, but becoming familiar with the maze of back roads that provide access may take a few trips. Coming from Johnson City the best route is to follow 19W and 11E north. Just before crossing the upper embayment of Boone Lake, turn onto Old Highway 11E to get to Bluff City. Highway 19E from Elizabethton also intersects Old Highwya 11E. Travelling from the Bristol area, take Highway 11E and 19 south to Bluff City

Overcast autumn and winter days bring on fantastic olive hatches.

to access the lower end of the river. Taking Highway 421 to Emmett Road will also allow access to the upper sections of the river near South Holston Dam.

Wading

The best access for waders is provided by TVA in the upper part of the river. Some of this is easily accessible from a parking lot, but most of the water requires a walk. This is one of the prettiest sections of the river, bounded only by woods and fields. Since this part of the river has so much access, the fish here see a lot of pressure. While the fishing can be difficult, it can also be rewarding. Expect to spend a lot of time changing flies as you work risers. Some days you may find a pattern that consistently get takes; other days it seems that one fish will eat a dry fly, the next only an emerger, and yet another fish is taking nymphs just under the surface. This river is truly a treat for the fisherman that likes to cast his fly to a specific rising fish.

Access is also available at the right-of-way at Hickory Tree and Weaver Pike bridges. There are also several roadside pull-offs along Hickory Tree Road that give waders good access. Look for water to rise at Hickory Tree Bridge approximately 90 minutes after South Holston Dam begins to

Large wild rainbows also spawn in the South Holston.

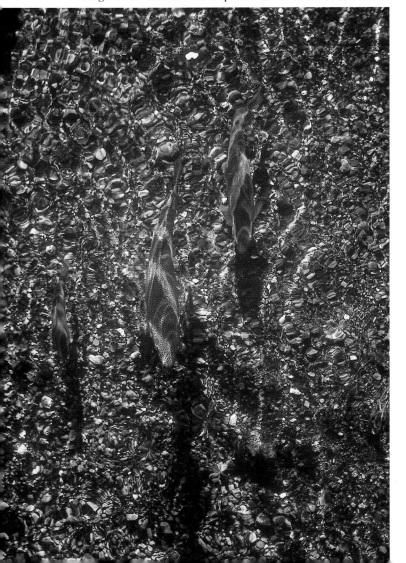

Colorful wild browns are common in the South Holston.

release water. Start watching for rising water at Weaver Pike bridge approximately 3 hours after scheduled releases.

Floating

Drift boats and rafts are both serviceable when the turbine is running water. However, any craft that is used will need an anchor to fish the river effectively. There are only three public ramps on the South Holston unless you can make arrangements with a landowner that has a gently sloping bank. This limits floating options but the fishing is often good enough on a float trip that you will probably enjoy a float of the entire river if daylight permits.

Floating the river really isn't an option if no water is being generated. Even canoes and pontoons will spend a lot of time dragging in a number of areas. As a result, floating is usually at its low point during the winter. Generation is often at a minimum and water levels are so low that boats will spend a considerable amount of time dragging bottom. May, June, and July are probably the best months to float the South Holston, with June being the very best. Fish that waders find so fussy during low flows will come to a fly more willingly with stronger currents.

Drift boats or rafts can be launched from Emmet Road at the bridge that crosses the river below South Holston Dam. The most popular public takeout is at Bluff City. Plan on rowing a little bit of Boone Lake to make the ramp. The least-used ramp on the river is at Weaver Pike bridge. While the ramp is serviceable, parking is virtually non existent. This would serve best as a launch site and have your vehicle immediately moved to your take-out.

Alternatives

If generation schedules aren't optimal you might check to see what the schedule is for the Watauga. You can be there in about thirty minutes. The Fort Patrick Henry tailwater is also nearby. There are also several freestone streams in the area that you might explore if TVA's generation schedules don't fit yours. Beaverdam Creek, Laurel Fork, and Doe River are only a few of the streams you might consider.

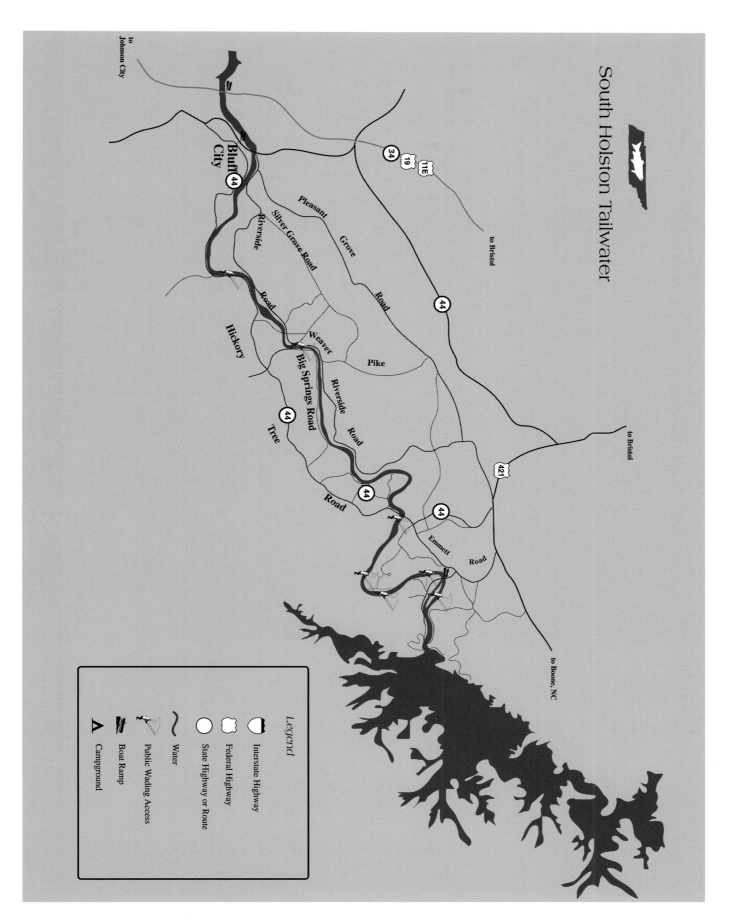

South Holston Tailwater

Legend

◖	Interstate Highway
⬢	Federal Highway
◯	State Highway or Route
∼	Water
⋎	Public Wading Access
⫽	Boat Ramp
⋀	Campground

The Watauga is among the most comfortable of the tail-waters to fish. The river never seems to be too big or too small. While there is enough access to spread fishermen out, the river is also floatable under a variety of conditions. Most of the access is due to the Watauga's somewhat urban setting, flowing through the middle of Elizabethton. At first glance, the Watauga closely resembles a large Appalachian freestone trout stream. In fact, wild trout flourish here and spawn successfully. The Watauga is also the only Tennessee tailwater that has brookies. They were introduced in 2000. TWRA's using the Watauga to see if brookies will holdover in Tennessee's tailwater fisheries.

While the Watauga tailwater flows from Wilbur Lake, it's Watauga Lake that is responsible for the cold water. Watauga Lake is a deep lake in the far northeast corner of Tennessee. Water remains cold in its depths, and is pulled through a turbine at Watauga Dam into Wilbur Lake. There is also a powerhouse at Wilbur Dam. Wilbur Lake is very small and very cold. It also hosts trout, more information can be found in the section that covers lakes on page 85.

Insect populations are more diverse in this river than most other tailwaters. A number of freestone tributaries and the tailwater's highly-oxygenated flow have provided the Watauga with a wide array of aquatic trout foods. This can make the task of fly selection not so critical as it can be on other tailwaters. The largest fish will often be the most selective, but smaller fish will often take common attractor patterns. Many of the best trout are caught on streamers. This is one of the few tailwaters where large nymphs can be effective. While most fishermen prefer small nymph and midge patterns, a few mountain boys still catch some nice fish on the same stonefly patterns they use up in the creeks.

The Watauga fishes well during winter but the best hatches of the year are typically in May and June. Caddis and Sulphurs are usually at their thickest during these months. Hatches continue through the summer, and crane flies are also important. A small, sparsely-dressed Sulphur pattern can pass for a crane fly in a pinch. Midges are a year-round hatch, but are most important during the cooler months when little else is hatching. The Watauga may be the best tailwater to fish terrestrial patterns in the summer. Beetle patterns are a favorite with float fishermen.

The Watauga is relatively easy to find since it flows through such a developed area. Driving up Interstate 81 from the south, take I-181 east through Johnson City. Exiting onto

The Watauga is synonymous with nice browns.

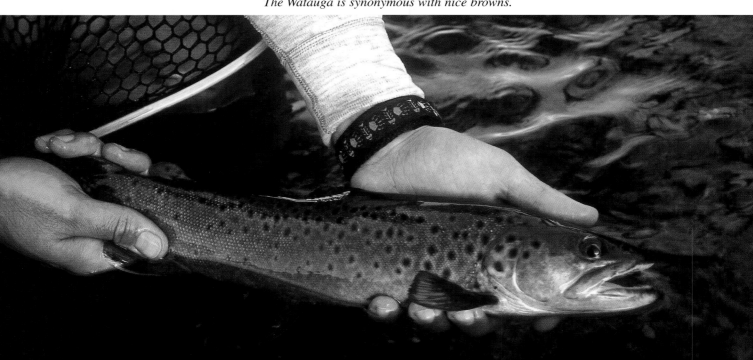

Boaters often share the river with waders when the river is off.

Highway 321 north to Elizabethton is generally the best way, but TN 91 can also get you there from I-181. Those travelling from the north may also prefer to come in via Johnson City as Highway 19 leads south from Bristol. South of Bristol Highway 19 divides into 19E and 19W. If you want to go directly into Elizabethton, take 19E. Highway 19W crosses both the Watauga and South Holston arms of Boone Lake. About four miles after crossing the South Holston, look for Piney Flats Road on the left. This will lead you to the small community of Watauga and the lower end of the river.

Wading

Wading access is good up and down the river, although not totally open. Wading is possible and popular at all the boat ramps. Hunter Bridge and Blevins Bend are among the most popular. There is also limited access near Siam Bridge. Personal pontoon watercraft can really open up wading opportunities, but a shuttle is required. These are surprisingly easy to arrange, though. Check with local fly shops for the most reliable shuttles.

Wading access is also available at the industrial park. While the surroundings are somewhat atypical of quality trout water, the fishing is superb. Access is also possible in the quality zone off Smalling Road which parallels the river. A campground in this section also has nice river frontage.

Waders near Hunter should watch for the river to rise about two or two and a half hours after the generators begin to push water. Rising water usually reaches the lower areas downstream of Blevins Bend in the neighborhood of five hours or less, depending on your location.

Floating

Floating the Watauga is possible during all phases of generation, but there are limitations. Fishing is usually at its best with zero generation, but this makes for very shallow water in some spots, particularly the area between Hunter and the powerhouse. Rafts or small pontoons are often preferred because they can be dragged over shallow shoals easier. However, drift boats do fine in many sections of the river, especially further downstream of Elizabethton. You will also prefer a craft that can employ an anchor if you are floating under generation. Otherwise you may only get a few shots at the best runs. Continue on with "You will have a wide range of opportunities when floating with one generator. Fish still rise in a good number of places, and nymphs provide plenty of action. Streamers also become more effective under these conditions, and are a good choice if there is a lull in insect activity.

I remember a trip my wife Charity and I took with a guide several years back on the Watauga. As we shoved off from the launch at Hunter that April morning, he explained that it would be several hours before any bugs might hatch. "Hopefully we'll get some caddis this afternoon, along with a couple of Sulphurs and olives. Up to that point you've got the choice of fishing nymphs or streamers." I imagined sitting in the raft, bobbing down the river just watching a bright orange indicator floating alongside. Then I thought about slapping a big Double Bunny streamer against the bank and stripping it in as big trout boiled on it in hot pursuit. I was about to announce my intentions of tying on a streamer when Charity announced, "Streamers... That's the way you catch the big ones." Our guide grinned and replied, "My kinda woman," as he worked the raft into position.

Guides prefer to fish streamers with sink-tip lines. This will ensure that the fly gets down to where it will be effective, and stays there. Sculpin imitations are a good choice

This small brown is likely to get large in the Watauga's waters.

Wild rainbows and browns are common in the Watauga.

since the river is full of them. These small fish spend all their time on the bottom, so that's another good reason to be sure your fly sinks well.

A midsummer float is ideal for slapping beetle and hopper imitations on the bank. This can be tough fishing, casting under tree branches. However, accomplished casters that aren't afraid of losing some flies will be rewarded with explosive strikes.

One of the most popular sections to float is the lower section of the river. Blevins Bend boat ramp is a good put in and there are two other boat ramps downstream. The first is a pay per use ramp at a campground along Smalling Road. The second is further down the river at the small community of Watauga.

Other good floats to consider are putting-in at Wilbur Dam and floating down to Hunter. You can also put-in at Hunter and float down to Blevins Bend. These are both casual floats that will allow you time to spend time fishing productive runs over the course of a day. The float from Hunter is the most urban stretch on the river, going through Elizabethton. It is also arguably the most productive stretch on the river, with some truly great riffles and runs broken up by long pools that undoubtedly harbor some beasts.

Alternatives

If the generation schedule on the Watauga is not good, consider the South Holston or the Fort Patrick Henry tailwater. The South Holston is the preferred choice of these two alternates, but beggers can't be choosers. Several freestone streams are also close by. Stony Creek, a freestone tributary, is only minutes from most sections of the Watauga. Doe River and Laurel Fork are approximately thirty minutes away. Beaverdam Creek is another spot to keep in mind if you can't get on the Watauga. One last option would be to check out Wilbur Lake, especially if you have a personal pontoon craft or belly boat on hand. It is very close, and might save the day if everything else is blown out.

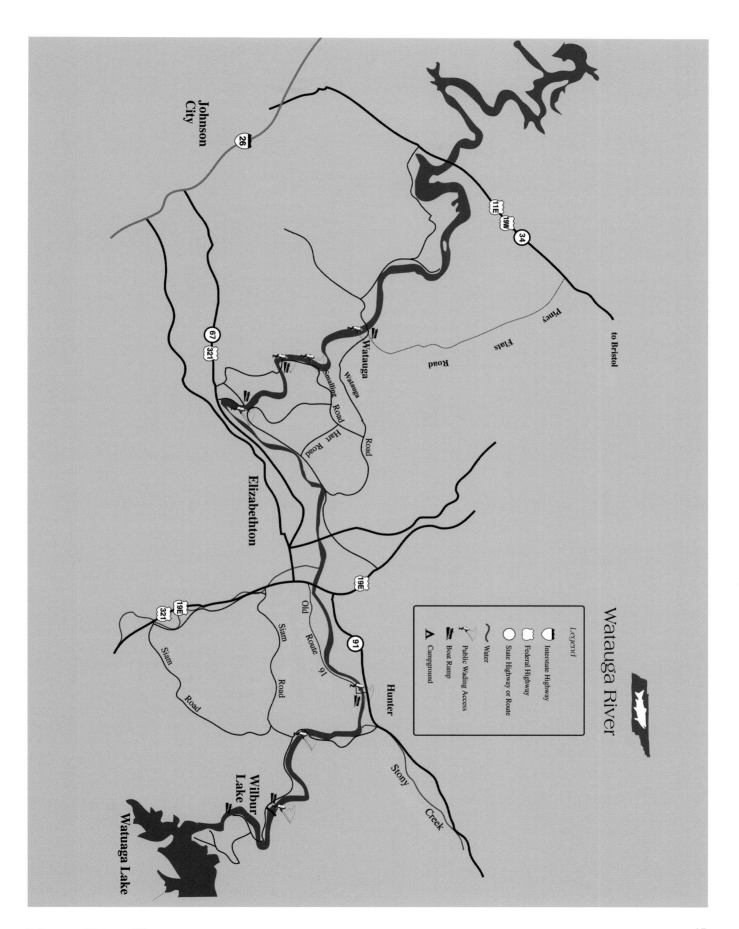

Watauga River

Legend

○ State Highway or Route
⬭ Federal Highway
◐ Interstate Highway

〜 Water
⚑ Public Wading Access
⚓ Boat Ramp
▲ Campground

Johnson City

26

67 321

Elizabethton

19E

19E 321

Siam Road

Siam Road

Old Route 91

91

Hunter

Stony Creek

Wilbur Lake

Watuaga Lake

Watauga

Watauga Road

Smalling Road

Harr Road

Piney Flats Road

11E
19W
34

to Bristol

Freestone Stream Fishing

The mountains of east Tennessee provide some of the most rewarding trout fishing to be found anywhere. Most of the trout water is in the Cherokee National Forest or the Great Smoky Mountains National Park. This means these waters are on public lands and access is generally not an issue. Fishing in the freestone streams is often a more private experience than casting on a tailwater. Even though the streams are far smaller, fishermen can spread out over a greater distance. Conversely, the tailwaters usually run across private land and large numbers of fishermen have to make do with only a few public access points. Usually the biggest access issues are based on how far you're willing to walk. There are plenty of streams that are accessible along a road. However, there are many more miles of stream only available for the fisherman with a stout set of legs.

Fly selection is not as crucial on these streams as it can be on the tailwaters. While the tailwaters have an incredible density of aquatic foods, the diversity is low. The freestoners are far less fertile which means that food is not nearly as available. However, the diversity of aquatic food is almost unparalleled anywhere else. There is an astounding variety of mayflies, caddisflies, stoneflies, midges, and craneflies in addition to salamanders, crayfish, and minnows. Mountain trout see food with less frequency which keeps them hungry. Additionally, there is a good chance that each morsel might be completely different from the one that came before. Water conditons are usually swift and choppy. That means that a trout might only get a fleeting glimpse at what an angler has to offer. As a result, bushy colorful fly patterns often work better than small subdued patterns that are usually tougher for a trout to see in such conditions. Showy attractors are often more productive because hungry trout can see them. Furthermore, fishermen see them better, get better drifts and miss fewer strikes.

Nymph patterns are highly effective in the mountain streams. However, most of the fishermen you'll find on these streams will be fishing dry flies. Even when dries aren't as effective as nymphs, there is still a good chance that a few trout will come to the dry. Nymph fishermen that use strike indicators sometimes switch to a dry fly because more trout are taking the indicator than the nymph!

Fishing in the mountains can be more strenuous than fishing the tailwaters. Trout in the mountains deal with a number of predators that tailwater trout can avoid. Many tailwater trout grow fast enough that kingfishers can't prey on them after a couple of months. Freestone trout may still be dodging kingfishers most of their lives. Even if they've outgrown the threat, they've lived with it so long they don't realize that they have. Since the trout are extremely skittish, they are often completely spooked after a few casts. Experienced fishermen often realize they have unintentionally spooked a pool before they cast their line.

Moving from pool to pool is the only way to stay on fresh fish.

The lack of food in the creeks makes for trout that have a smaller average size than what is found in the tailwaters. Trout caught in the tailwaters are rarely under nine inches, and may average over a foot long. Nine-inch trout are generally a bit better than average in the mountain streams. Of course, the size of the stream can have a direct correlation to the size of the trout you might find. Large brown trout are far more common in large streams like Little River and Tellico River than they are in small streams.

The size of trout in freestone streams also brings up the topic of stocked and wild trout. Finglerling trout are rarely stocked in the streams. Trout of at least nine inches and ranging to about thirteen inches are more typical. Stocked trout will occasionally be over 16 inches, and may be well over 20. Most trout stocked in the streams are rainbows. Wild rainbow trout rarely grow over twelve inches long in east Tennessee streams. In fact, very few grow over nine inches long. This is mostly a function of a less-than-ideal food base coupled with their affinity for swift currents. If you are fishing a stream like Citico Creek or Laurel Fork that receives regular visits from a state stocking truck and catch several rainbows between 14 -16 inches it is almost certain that they were hatchery fish.

Stocked rainbows can be relatively easy to catch for a number of reasons. The most notable reason is that stockers have grown up with humans feeding them and are unaware of the dangers posed by fishermen. They may also feed a bit more aggressively and attack unrealistic patterns. Once a stocked trout hits the stream, it has to figure out what to eat. It might take them a while to figure out what food is since they are fed a diet of trout chow not mayfly nymphs and caddis larvae. Nymphs and streamers with a lot of flash are among the most effective flies when the stocking truck comes to town. Even after these trout have lived in the stream for a few weeks, they are still likely to get caught. The reason is that they have to eat a good deal to nourish their large bodies. In many instances, large, stocked trout will never be as healthy as they were the day they were stocked. Hunger can make a trout do stupid things.

There are a number of relatively small trout that are tougher to catch than large, stocked trout. These will be wild trout. There are plenty of streams with strictly wild populations of trout. There are usually good populations of wild trout in streams that are stocked as well. TWRA (Tennessee Wildlife Resources Agency) stocks these streams so that catch rates will be bolstered. Research has indicated that bait fishermen do little to affect wild trout populations in Tennessee's freestone streams. Very few wild fish are fooled by corn or scented putty baits. Most of those that are caught are deemed to small by fishermen and thrown back.

Brown trout are a bit different from rainbows. It is not uncommon for wild, stream-bred brown trout to grow as long in freestone streams as they will in the tailwaters. However, the tailwater fish will almost always outweigh their freestone cousins. Browns tend to reside in calmer waters than rainbows and this gives them an edge in these streams where food is not plentiful. This means that they are not wasting calories holding in swift currents unless there is plenty of food moving in the flow. Also, once a brown trout gets to be nine or ten inches it will begin to prey on sculpins, dace, and crayfish. Preying on larger food items allows these fish to grow large and eat less often. Most fishermen hunting for a trophy brown will fish with oversized fly patterns. This can be a good tactic, but don't forget that most fish can't afford to pass up a meal in these streams and most of these big boys didn't get that way by being choosy. These brown trout grew large by a combination of eating well, finding a pool that has feeding lanes close to cover, and hiding at the first sign of danger.

Catching a big fish is always a thrill but many fishermen don't feel like a trout has to be large to be worth catching. Most fishermen that frequent Tennessee's mountain streams are looking for something more than large trout. Ask any dedicated mountain fisherman for a trout he was proud of and he will likely add a few tough, yet small trout to his largest catch. Making a tough cast in tight cover is sometimes reward enough. Generally speaking, seasoned mountain fishermen feel that a wild trout of about ten inches is pretty good and a trout over twelve inches is excellent. Wild rainbows rarely get bigger than this. A good stream with wild brown trout will have a decent number reaching fourteen inches. Browns over 16 inches are relatively rare although the best streams may have several that might exceed 24 inches.

Stream flows are far more predictable in these streams than they will be on the tailwaters. On most days a fisherman can just get in his car and drive to a stream and it will be fishable. Only foolish tailwater fishermen leave home without checking generation schedules. There are times though, when stream flows can definitely make it tough if not impossible to get any fishing in. Tennessee's mountain streams are particularly prone to flooding. There will be several high-water events during the course of a season, and every few years there are catastrophic floods. A good number of streams experienced one such flood in the spring of 1994. Flows hit record levels and completely destroyed roads in the Little River, Tellico River, and Citico Creek watersheds. While such floods are uncommon, you should expect high water if heavy rains have moved through. Most of the time high water will pass in as little as a few hours, and rarely last longer than a day or so. A good strategy to deal with high water is to "run and gun" your way up and down the river only hitting those spots which are fishable. These conditions typically call for big nymphs or streamers. Tributary streams often run-off first, and may not be high at all. Isolated storms will often dump several inches of rain on a watershed, but leave adjacent watersheds untouched. This is usually a summertime event and it pays to check out tributaries or a stream just over the ridge.

Rainbow trout are the most common of Tennessee's trout species. They are widely distributed and it is relatively rare to find a stretch of suitable trout stream where they are not found. Brown trout are fairly common and overlap rainbows in a number of creeks and streams. The swift-flowing waters of Tennessee's mountain streams are an ideal home for the rainbow. They were introduced in the 1920s and are still stocked in many streams on a regular basis. They are eager to rise and seem to have a preference for aquatic insects over minnows and larger prey. Stocked rainbows rarely gain the stream smarts of their wild counterparts and are often too aggressive for their own good.

There are very few streams where browns are the sole game fish. In fact, when they do occur with rainbows they are often in the minority. They will, however, grow the largest. Browns are seldom picky about their food in these streams, eating everything from midges and mayflies to crayfish, salamanders, and other trout. Typically caught in the 6- to 10-inch range, they can be expected to reach 13 inches in even the smallest creeks. Large streams regularly grow a few brown trout measured more accurately in pounds than inches. Most fishermen don't realize just how plentiful brown trout are in streams where they occur. They are extremely shy and cautious by nature. Stocked browns seem to exhibit more common sense than stocked rainbows. Wild browns in Appalachian streams are notoriously secretive. Fisheries biologists have often commented that managing for large wild browns is tough to do since they seem to do best left alone. More than one biologist has commented that the average brown trout is smarter than the average fisherman.

Brook trout are the only native salmonids in Tennessee. Known to the mountain people as "specs", they once ranged throughout the state's high-elevation freestone streams, but their numbers have fallen during the past century. Logging operations that denuded the mountains took a toll on the streams. Many were choked with silt from the bare, gullied hillsides. Introduced rainbow trout seem to have replaced brookies in many of streams where they were decimated. Tennessee's forests have regenerated and many brook trout poplulations are safe, while others are being restored. Fishermen that find a brook trout on their line will almost always be higher than 2500 feet in elevation. There are very few populations lower than that. As a result, brookies are restricted to small streams which, in turn, restrict their growth. Seasoned Appalachian anglers are proud of a spec that is ten inches long. Few will achieve that size, and even fewer grow larger. Brookies that are native to Tennessee are actually a sub-species. Southern Appalachian brook trout have similar features to northern brookies but are generally more colorful, exhibiting more red. They are also more prolific, inhabiting every wet spot in a creek. They rarely grow over eight inches long, though. Northern brook trout have been stocked in Tennessee and there are a few populations that have held. Biologists have compared these fish to the native southern brookies and found that while they will often grow larger than eight inches, their populations are more sparse.

Abrams Creek Watershed

Abrams Creek

SIZE 5-10

Abrams Creek has long been recognized as one of the best wild trout streams in the Southeast. It drains the Cades Cove area of the Great Smoky Mountains which has a geologic base composed of limestone. This moderates the generally acidic water typical of the southern Appalachians to make this one of the most fertile freestones in Tennessee. Aquatic insect populations are high, and that translates into a good trout population. As a result, Abrams Creek rainbows may be a bit more selective than trout in other streams. While they rarely hone in on only one fly pattern, they may be thinking of one insect in particular.

Abrams Creek is one of only a few streams I know where a profusion of insects might hatch with nary a trout rising. It is extremely frustrating to tie on a nymph while brushing mayflies out of your face. Tailwater and spring-creek fishermen tend to find good success on Abrams. This is probably a result of their willingness to tie on small nymphs rather than stick with the bushy Wulff-style dry flies favored by many creek fishermen.

Baitfish populations are also high in Abrams Creek, and small creek shiners will give the dry-fly fisherman fits. Remember that these small fish only get to eat what the trout allow them. Either switch to a nymph or fish different types of water. Streamers are a good option to catch trout while excluding pesky minnows.

Only a handful of runs can be fished without losing sight of your car, so fishing Abrams Creek is really a hike-in affair. Focus your trout fishing efforts on the water most accessible from Cades Cove, this is the best water on the stream. Many fishermen including myself have fished the water near the Abrams Creek Campground for trout with little or no success. This stretch of water is a coolwater fishery that is mostly inhabited by smallmouth bass. There is plenty of backcountry water that is completely neglected, though. The water between Abrams Falls and the backcountry campsite at Little Bottoms is top notch, yet rarely fished. This is tough water to reach and deters all but the most determined trout fishermen.

Dawn over Cades Cove in the Great Smoky Mountains.

There are a number of nice wild rainbows in Abrams Creek.

There are two horseshoe bends upstream of Abrams Falls that swing away from the trail. Both of these sections of the stream are locally famous for their trout and lost fishermen. If you do fish one of these horseshoes it is advisable that you start early in the day and keep moving. Do not leave the stream to find the trail, that is how most fishermen get lost. Stay in the stream and keep going until it rejoins the stream, or turn around and get out where you got in.

Abrams Creek is a good stream to keep in mind at any time of the year. Since much of its flow originates from subterranean aquifers, it maintains a more stable water temperature than other creeks. It is typically warmer than other local streams in the winter and cooler in the summer. If water conditions are high, try one of Abrams' tributaries in Cades Cove. There are many times when one may be very fishable while other streams are blown out.

Coming in from the south or west, take Highway 321 to Townsend. There are signs every step of the way from Townsend that will lead you to Cades Cove. Coming from the north you may take 321 south from Pigeon Forge to Townsend. This will be quicker than fighting traffic the entire length of Pigeon Forge and Gatlinburg to enter the park.

Anthony Creek
SIZE 2

Anthony Creek is full of little rainbows but will be a challenge for anyone not acclimated to small-stream tactics. Much of this stream is hidden in rhododendron tangles but anyone willing to walk a bit can find plenty of spots to drop a fly. Most of the best water is in the Cades Cove picnic area. However, this is only practical to fish in the off-season. Nice weather will fill this stretch with picnickers and rock-skippers.

Forge Creek
SIZE 2-3

Forge Creek is a great little trout stream that is completely overshadowed by Abrams Creek which it feeds. While conditions are somewhat tight, there is still a good helping of casting room for a stream this size. Access is good along Forge Creek Road at the back of Cades Cove and continues along the Gregory Ridge Trail.

Mill Creek
SIZE 2

Mill Creek is a small stream that merges with Abrams Creek at the Abrams Falls trailhead. It loses significant volume upstream of its confluence with Forge Creek. Its rainbows are generally small but fun to mess around with. This stream is usually ignored by most fishermen who almost always pick Abrams Creek when they arrive in Cades Cove.

Black bears are common in Cades Cove.

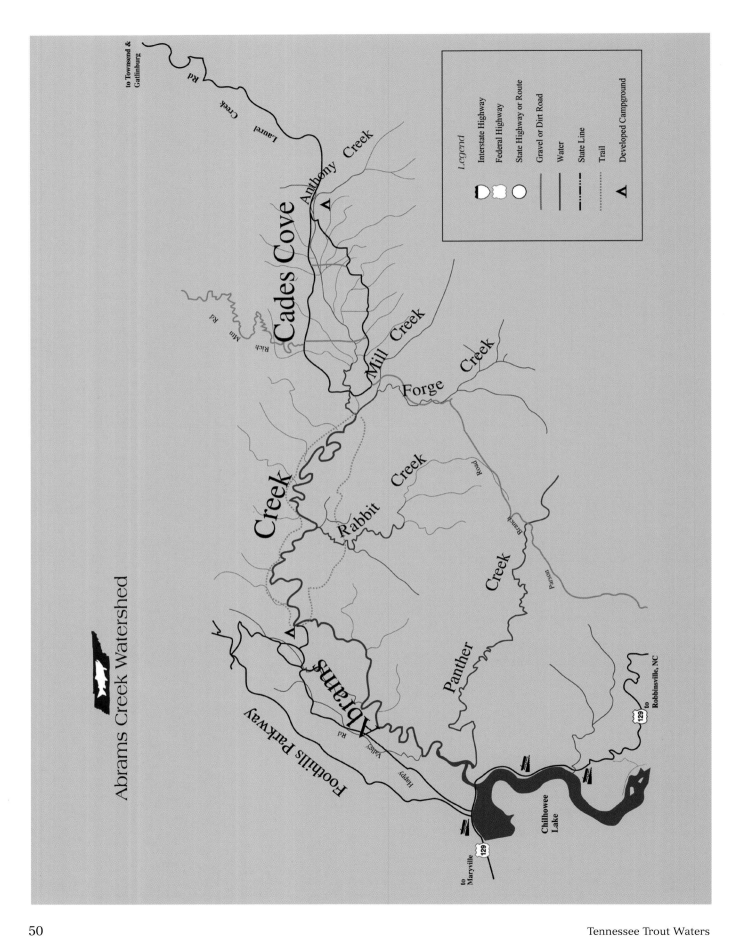

Abrams Creek Watershed

Freestone Streams
Beaverdam Creek and Laurel Creek Watersheds

This section gives Beaverdam Creek top billing even though it is not the main stream in the watershed. Laurel Creek is actually the main flow of the watershed, draining Beaverdam Creek as well as other streams in Virginia. Most Virginians treat the state line like the Great Wall of China, rarely venturing into Tennessee to fish Beaverdam or the southern, upstream area of the Laurel Creek system. Most Virginians stay to the north, fishing White Top Laurel, another branch of the Laurel Creek watershed. In fact, Laurel Creek is much better known by Virginians, while most Tennessee fly-anglers rarely venture beyond its main southern tributary, Beaverdam Creek.

Beaverdam Creek
SIZE 6-8

Beaverdam Creek's headwaters are far different from most other southern Appalachian streams. The creek begins in Shady Valley, a mountain cove tucked between Holston

Beaverdam Creek.

Mountain and Iron Mountain. This is farm country and the stream flows across fields resembling an irrigation ditch on Montana's high plains. Shady Valley looks like a modern-day version of historic Cades Cove in Great Smoky Mountains National Park. Beaverdam Creek is essentially inaccessible through Shady Valley as it is surrounded by private land. However, according to TWRA, this is not very productive water and trout populations are relatively low.

As Beaverdam Creek falls from Shady Valley and rushes toward Virginia it enters the Cherokee National Forest and begins to take on the character of an Appalachian trout stream. Long, wide-open flats are left behind and replaced with boulders, pocket water, and choppy riffles. The stream is chock full of wild rainbow and brown trout. Beaverdam's waters are a bit more fertile than other streams in the region. Perhaps this is a result of the fertilizers used on farms in Shady Valley. No matter, it can sometimes be tough to tell wild and stocked rainbows apart. I've caught several rainbows that were too pretty to have come from a stocking truck but I couldn't quite convince myself that they were wild, either. There may be a good number of stockers holding over, but I also suspect that a few rainbows grow to twelve or thirteen inches on their own.

While there are plenty of rainbows, brown trout are what most fishermen come looking for. Beaverdam Creek is known as a top producer for larger-than-average browns. The stream may not look that different from others in Tennessee but there is definitely a combination of food and habitat that grows some nice trout. Even though there are good numbers of large brown trout in Beaverdam, don't expect them to come to a fly any quicker than they might anywhere else. Runoff from the farms in Shady Valley keeps the water tinged most of the time though, and this can be a big help. The water will almost surely be muddy after it rains. Be sure to take care as you wade. Silt that stains the water will also make the rocks slicker than average.

Access is relatively straight forward downstream of Shady Valley as Beaverdam Creek is shadowed by TN 133. The route from Elizabethton is scenic, driving up Stony Creek into Shady Valley. Take TN 91 from Elizabethton and Hunter over the mountain into Shady Valley. Drive through a four-way stop and the road will change to TN 133 and lead to Beaverdam Creek. This may not be the quickest route, though. Some find it easier to take I-81 to the Hwy 11 exit near Abingdon, Virginia and follow Hwy 58 to Damascus. From Damascus, it's only a short drive across the Tennessee border and up Beaverdam Creek.

Primitive camping is available at Backbone Rock where there is a Forest Service campground. Backbone Rock is the most distinctive feature along Beaverdam Creek. Backbone Rock is a long, narrow rock spur that juts from Holston Mountain. The road passes through a narrow tunnel blasted through the rock.

The Beaverdam Creek watershed is fairly narrow and there is not a well-developed system of large tributaries.

*Beaverdam has an excellent brown trout population,
with several breaking the 16-inch mark.*

However, there are several small streams that can provide some additional fishing opportunities. Laurel Creek is only about twenty to thiry minutes, away and is an excellent alternate to fish. This will require a drive to Damascus, Virginia. Turn east on Highway 58 and look for TN 91 to Laurel Bloomery and Mountain City, Tennessee. Stony Creek is another good freestoner to check out near Elizabethton, but the Watauga tailwater might be more productive if TVA's schedule meshes with yours.

Birch Branch
SIZE 1

Birch Branch is an excellent small tributary of Beaverdam Creek. Rainbows are present but this stream has a strong population of small, native brookies that outumbers them. Access should be fine but the lowest half mile of the stream is on private property so show proper courtesy.

Fagall Branch
SIZE 1-2

Fagall Branch may be the best of Beaverdam Creeks's small tributaries. Rainbows and a few brown trout will be caught in the downstream portions of the stream, but brookies begin to outnumber them as you go upstream. This may have the best brook trout fishing in the Beaverdam Creek watershed.

Laurel Creek
SIZE 3-5

Laurel Creek is a relatively unknown trout fishery in upper east Tennessee. There are a number of reasons why few fishermen are aware of it, but the quality of fishing should not be one of them. Laurel Creek is in a somewhat isolated corner of the state that is hard to reach if you never leave Tennessee. However, if you venture a few miles north into Virginia the stream is easily reached by driving south from Damascus. Driving toward

Damascus forces fishermen to drive past the South Holston and Watauga tailwaters before driving about ten miles alongside Beaverdam Creek. Perhaps there are too many temptations for the average fisherman to ever reach Laurel Creek.

Beaverdam Creek is actually a tributary of Laurel Creek. They converge in Damascus and eventually flow into the South Fork of the Holston River. Whitetop Laurel Creek also enters the flow and making Laurel Creek a sizeable mountain river as it flows west along Virginia's southern border. Some of the best water is inside Tennessee, though. Roadside access is best close to the state line. While the stocking truck makes regular visits in the spring, there is an excellent population of wild trout. In fact, neighboring Beaverdam Creek can only top Laurel Creek with scenery and overall access. Laurel Creek is closely shadowed by TN 91, but much of it is on private property.

In spite of the creek's close proximity to the highway, it's scenery is still beautiful. One of the most colorful communities in Tennessee, Laurel Bloomery, is situated on Laurel Creek's headwaters. Rhododendron, catawba rhododendron, flame azalea, and mountain laurel all bloom in profusion every May and June in this corner of the state.

Like Beaverdam Creek, much of the upper reaches of Laurel Creek flow through agricultural country. This causes a somewhat silty bottom and slightly dirty water clarity, making for prime nymph and streamer fishing. Wade with caution, though, there are a number of sloped rock ledges in the

Backbone Rock

stream and the micro layer of silt makes them extremely slick. There are a number of tributaries but Gentry Creek is the only one with much public access.

To reach Laurel Creek from Elizabethton, drive up Stony Creek into Shady Valley. Take TN 91 from Elizabethton and Hunter over the mountain into Shady Valley. Drive through a four-way stop and the road will change to TN 133 and lead to Beaverdam Creek. Try to ignore Beaverdam and drive on to Damascus, Virginia. Take Highway 58 east for about two miles before taking TN 91 up Laurel Creek toward Mountain City, Tennessee. This may not be the quickest route, though, some find it easier to take I-81 to the Hwy 11 exit near Abingdon, Virginia and follow Hwy 58 to Damascus. From Damascus, it's only a short drive across the Tennessee border and up Laurel Creek.

Gentry Creek
SIZE 1-3

Gentry Creek is mostly composed of rainbow trout with a few browns in the mix. However, once a fisherman walks up the trail at the end of the road, brook trout will begin to turn up. If you go far enough, you'll find a waterfall that blocks the upstream movement of rainbows and only brookies are present. Conditions are pretty tight above the falls, but we can always dream of a whopper in the plunge pool. The waterfall is about two and half miles upstream from the trailhead. A fishermen hiking in felt-soled boots will probably do better than a hiker wearing hiking boots. The trail crosses the creek an inordinate number of times.

To find Gentry Creek, take a left turn off TN 91 as you drive up Laurel Creek. Look for Hawkins Road. Turn right onto West Hawkins Road and follow it to the end of the road at the trailhead.

Kate Branch
SIZE 1

Kate Branch is a small tributary of Gentry Creek. You will likely find yourself alone on this stream with only small native brookies to keep you company. To find Kate Branch, drive to the end of the road along Gentry Creek. Follow the trail upstream to the point where the trail forks. Take the right fork up Kate Branch, but beware, the trail is about as overgrown as the creek. You will cross one small tributary of Gentry Creek before reaching Kate Branch.

Gilbert Branch
SIZE 1

Gilbert Branch is a small tributary of Gentry Creek that converges upstream of the waterfall. A trail follows this stream but don't expect much traffic. After passing the trail that follows Kate Branch, watch for the waterfall and another fork in the trail a bit beyond that. The right fork takes you up Gilbert Branch.

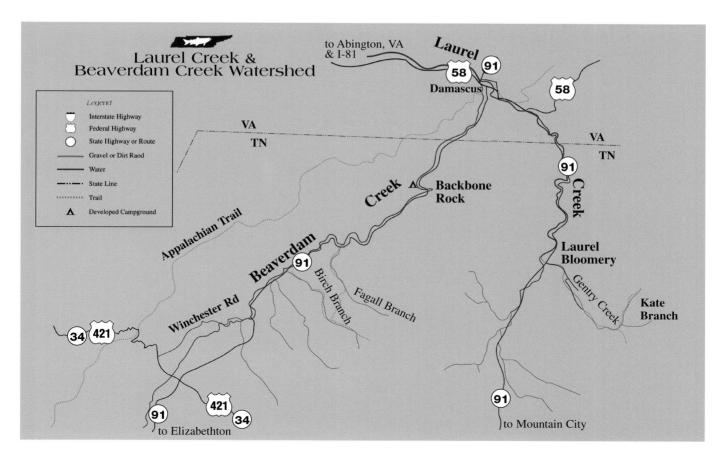

Citico Creek
SIZE 7-9

Citico Creek and its trout are found in some of Tennessee's most rugged territory. Citico once joined the flow of the famed Little Tennessee tailwater, and large rainbows and browns ran up it to spawn. However, the lower stretches of the stream are not a prime trout location. Summer temperatures are too warm to support a good population. Smallmouth bass are the predominant game fish in lower Citico Creek. There are, however, miles of quality trout water upstream of Little Citico Creek. While there is an excellent population of wild rainbows and browns, TWRA stocks Citico weekly between Little Citico Creek and the Citico Creek Wilderness boundary from mid-March through mid-September. The same permit required for Tellico River is also required for Citico Creek. The stream is also closed to fishing on Thursday and Friday during this period.

Nearly all of the creek runs parallel to the graveled Citico Creek Road. Several primitive Forest Service campgrounds on the stream make it an easy visit for anyone willing to camp. Be sure to have everything you need, though, you will be some distance from the nearest store. Weekends are extremely busy on Citico Creek during the season, but weekdays are relatively quiet. Fall is a great time when the weather is still nice and the crowds that follow the state stocking truck are gone for the season.

Typical bushy dry flies and bead-head nymphs will catch good numbers of fish. Stocked trout along the gravel road take flashy nymphs and streamers more often than dry flies. Holdovers that remain into the fall and winter begin rising to naturals and become better dry-fly targets. Most bait-fishers also have a tendency to fish only deep holes, so any stocked

Citico Creek.

fish that makes it's home in a riffle or section of pocket water is very likely to last more than a weekend in the creek.

While Citico can be rather crowded on a weekend, there is at least one stretch of water where you might find some privacy. There is a hairpin curve on the stream where it leaves the road and returns only a few yards from where it left. This a minimum of a half-day trip to fish. Any stockers you catch in this section of the creek are likely to be holdovers since there is no place for a state truck to dump fish; you are likely to find a good number of wild trout. In fact, many of the Citico locals will not fish this bend since it isn't stocked.

Citico Creek leaves the gravel road at a low concrete bridge that crosses over to a camping area known as the Warden Fields. The creek is only accessible via trail. The trailhead is actually located across the stream from the Warden Fields and can be accessed by not crossing the concrete bridge and taking the next turn. Be sure to have a vehicle with lots of clearance or you may bottom out. You may prefer not to drive the short distance to the trailhead and save some wear and tear on you vehicle. Less than a mile upstream of Warden Fields is the Citico Creek Wilderness boundary, and the creek's headwater forks are just a little way further.

Indian Boundary is a developed campground located just off the Cherohala Skyway. There is also a warmwater lake here. This campground provides an excellent place to camp that is only a short distance from Citico Creek and its tributaries, as well as the Tellico River system. In the event you find yourself in the Citico watershed and water conditions are high, make the short drive over the mountain to Tellico River. Conditions may be far better in this adjacent watershed.

Citico Creek is pretty well isolated and only travelling back roads will get you there. Coming from the north, take Highway 411 south. After crossing the bridge over Tellico Lake you will come into the small town of Vonore. Take a left turn onto Citico Road at one of the few stop lights in town. You will pass Fort Loudoun State Park shortly and you'll know you're on the right path. Stay on this road all the way to the stream and it will eventually turn to gravel. Coming from the south, the easiest route is to go to Vonore and take the right turn onto Citico Road. A few people prefer to turn onto Highway 68 toward Tellico Plains where it intersects 411 at Madisonville. At Tellico Plains get on the Cherohala Skyway to Indian Boundary. Coming down to the creek from Indian Boundary puts you in the uppermost part of the stream, and close to the North and South forks of Citico Creek.

Double Camp Creek
SIZE 2-4

Double Camp Creek is a surprisingly good stream that supports wild rainbows and browns. This stream is followed most

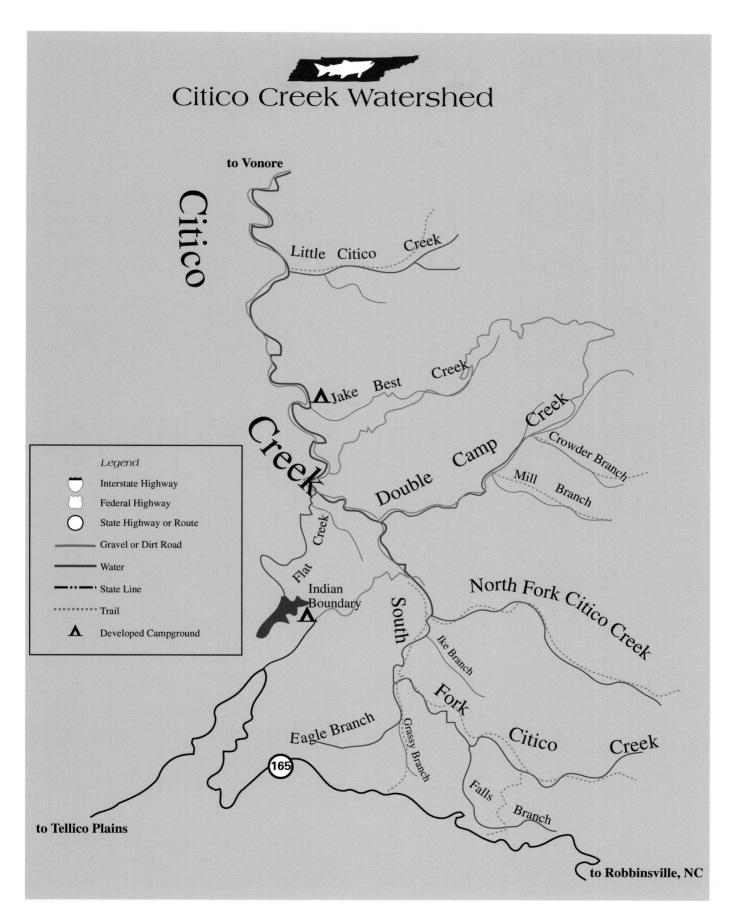

Citico Creek Watershed

to Vonore

Citico

Little Citico Creek

Creek

Jake Best Creek

Double Camp Creek

Crowder Branch

Mill Branch

Flat Creek

Indian Boundary

South Fork

North Fork Citico Creek

Ike Branch

Citico Creek

Eagle Branch

Grassy Branch

165

Falls Branch

to Tellico Plains

to Robbinsville, NC

Legend

	Interstate Highway
	Federal Highway
◯	State Highway or Route
———	Gravel or Dirt Road
———	Water
·—··—··	State Line
··········	Trail
▲	Developed Campground

TWRA stocks some nice rainbows in Citico Creek.

of its length by Double Camp Creek Road, Forest Service Road 59. There are several clearings along the creek which are used as primitive campsites. Some stocked rainbow trout may make it into the lower stretches of the creek. These are likely to be the only rainbows over twelve inches you will find, but the occasional large brown can provide a pleasant surprise.

Flat Creek
SIZE 2-3

This is an easy stream to miss if you drive by too fast. Flat Creek is a relatively small stream, but it can be rewarding for the fisherman willing to give it a try. There is a good population of wild rainbows in this stream and a brown could turn up at any time. You might be surprised to fish this modest little creek and catch several nice rainbows. A good number of stockers from Citico escape up this small stream. Many will pass their days unmolested, unlike their kin that probably found their way into a creel back in Citico Creek. There is no trail along this stream so you will travel via the stream bed.

North Fork Citico Creek
SIZE 3

The North Fork of Citico Creek is a superb rainbow-trout stream. The fish are typically small but are abundant. Fish over nine inches are fairly rare but, it's hard to find another stream with fish as greedy. If you're not catching trout on this stream, don't blame your fly. The trout will eat a variety of patterns but are scared of their own shadow. Only spooked trout won't inspect a fly that has a good drift. Brook trout are a possible catch, but only for the hardiest fishermen. There is a waterfall, Goat Falls, that has blocked rainbows from encroaching on a remnant population of native brookies in the highest reaches of the watershed.

South Fork Citico Creek
SIZE 3-4

South Fork is a bit larger than the neighboring North Fork. Rainbows are essentially the only species you will find here. Apparently browns found downstream in Citico Creek find the South Fork too rough for their liking. They are an extremely rare catch here. There are miles of water on the South Fork that go months between visits from fishermen. The trout, though small, are accordingly greedy.

South Fork drains a tight mountain valley known as Jeffrey's Hell. Back in the early 1900s, a bear hunter by the name of Jeffrey was running a bear with his pack of hounds when a forest fire broke out. Frantic to find his favorite hound he ran through the flames in spite of protests from his other hunting companions. Jeffrey's last comment was that he'd find his dog or go to hell trying. That was the last time he was seen and many locals still refer to the South Fork as Jeffrey's Hell. True small-stream fanatics may prefer to park on the Cherohala Skyway and hike the Jeffrey's Hell trail to the uppermost part of South Fork. Conditions can be tight in places but most casts that reach the water will be rewarded with a strike.

South Fork Citico Creek.

Tim Doyle photo

56

Cosby Creek Watershed

Cosby Creek
SIZE 2-4

Cosby Creek is one of the lesser-known streams in the Great Smoky Mountains National Park. For years most of it was closed to fishing to protect a native population of brook trout. However, the National Park Service opened areas of this stream in 2002 as part of an experiment. Fisheries biologists suspect that there are several reasons for the century-long decline of brookies in the southern Appalachians. They now believe that fishermen are far from the top of the list of most damaging factors. It's possible that this experiment will lead to the opening of all brook trout streams in the park.

The largest water on Cosby Creek is outside the park and is stocked with rainbows. Even though this stream is modest in size, a few fishermen catch 18-inch rainbows after the most charitable stockings. A few stockers will find their way into the national park but the population quickly reverts almost entirely to wild trout. Rainbows are the predominant catch up to the campground, but brookies begin to turn up with only a short walk. At this writing, none of Cosby Creek's tributaries are open to fishing. While they are small, they will increase fishing opportunities in this small watershed.

Brookies are typically small in this stream. Many hoped that there would be some trophies caught the first week the stream was opened after 27 years of no fishing. Very few fish break the seven-inch mark, but they are present in almost every damp spot in the creek bed. This seems to dash the theory that a lack of fishing pressure can produce big trout. Fisheries biologists are interested to see if size might increase with fishing pressure. Thinning out the population might mean more food and space for those brookies that aren't creeled.

Cosby Campground is one of the quietest in the national park, and is an excellent spot for the fisherman to consider. While Cosby Creek has limited opportunities, they are largely ignored. The Middle Prong of the Pigeon River is only about twenty or thirty minutes away and can exponentially increase your fishing possibilities.

From I-40, take the Highway 321 exit at Wilton Springs. Follow 321 south through Cosby. Highway 321 will make a right turn in Cosby toward Gatlinburg but you will go straight and the road will become TN 32. It's about two miles to the park entrance and another two miles up to the campground. If you're coming from Gatlinburg take Highway 321 north to Cosby. When you get to Cosby, take a right at the first stop and take TN 32 to the park entrance.

Indian Camp Creek
SIZE 2

Indian Camp Creek is another brook trout stream in the Cosby Creek watershed. Even local fishermen were somewhat unaware of this small stream until 2002. This stream in the Great Smoky Mountains National Park had been closed to fishing since the mid 1970s to protect its population of brook trout. This stream was chosen for experimental regulations by park biologists who believe that fishermen have little influence on the population structure of native brook trout. Fishermen that have sampled Indian Camp Creek admit that over 25 years of no fishing has had no beneficial effect on the size of its small brookies.

This small stream is easy to drive past if you're not paying attention. Several commercial campgrounds are available in the area where the creek flows under Highway 321.

Cosby Creek brookie.

Doe River
SIZE 4-7

The Doe River is among the very best freestone trout streams in Tennessee, and has something to offer just about any fly-fisherman. The stream is large in the lower elevations and is still medium size in the higher reaches before it splits into headwater tributaries. Some sections of the stream are somewhat isolated and require a hike. Others are easily accessed from the road and get regular visits from TWRA stocking trucks.

Doe River is a direct tributary of the Watauga River tailwater. However, this lowest stretch of the river gets a bit warm in the summer and is rarely targeted by trout fishermen. The best water to focus your efforts is upstream of Hampton. The Doe River gorge is legendary among local fishermen for its large browns. This is the most remote section of

Tying on at Doe River.

the river, if not the most dangerous. This is no place to be during high water or a flash flood. Above the gorge, the stream flows along Highway 19E. There are several pulloffs along the highway and some side roads but much of the stream is on private land. Smallmouth bass are also residents of Doe River and are present from this part of the creek all the way down to the Watauga River.

The best all-around stretch of water on Doe River is inside Roan Mountain State Park. Roan Mountain is renowned for its early summer displays of blooming laurels, rhododendrons, and flame azaleas. There is an extremely well-groomed campground in the park that will accommodate RV's as well as tents. Those looking for a mountain getaway without camping might be interested in one of the rental cabins inside the park. Roan Mountain State Park would make an excellent base to fish not only Doe River, but Laurel Fork, Beaverdam Creek, and the Watauga tailwater.

Doe River stays a good size even as it ascends in elevation. This keeps water temperatures cool even in the summer and probably accounts for the abundance of better-than-average brown trout. Skilled fishermen often look to the waters inside Roan Mountain State Park for their best shot at a good brown. Some even believe that a few look forward to eating nine-inch trout stocked by the state. While only the very largest and rarest brown trout might do that, a few more browns of about 14-16 inches are caught from Doe River than other comparably sized creeks in Tennessee.

Rainbows are common up and down the river. Rainbows are stocked frequently, but most trout in the stream are wild. Wild brookies are even caught in the uppermost reaches of Doe River. They begin to turn up around the campground. In fact, it is likely you might catch a grand slam of browns, rainbows, and brookies in the park.

Native brookies still hold on in the highest reaches of Doe River.

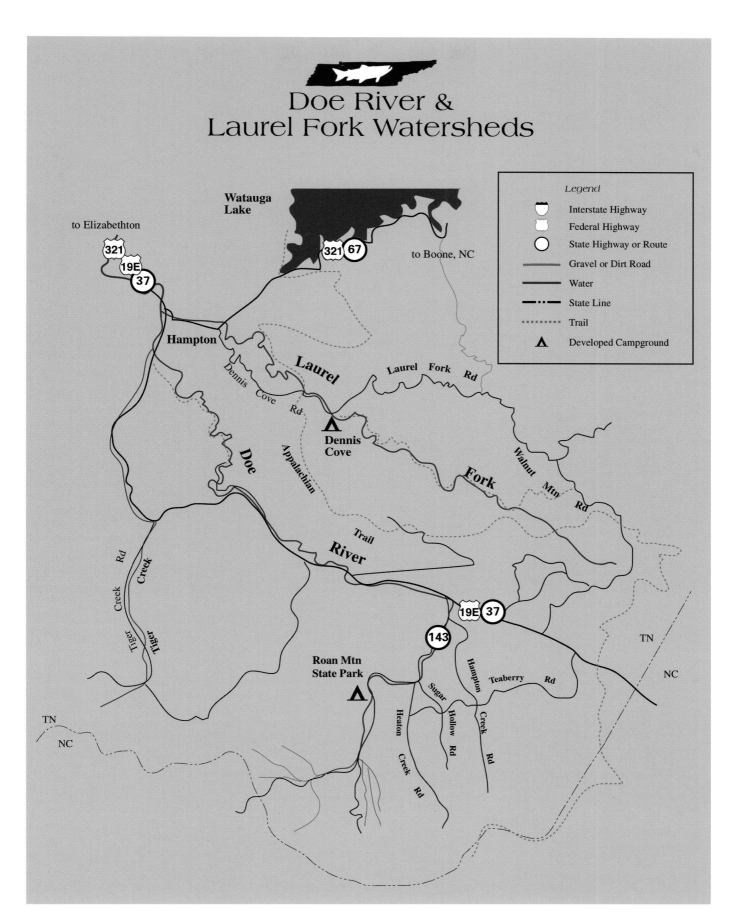

Doe River &
Laurel Fork Watersheds

Watauga Lake

to Elizabethton

321
19E
37

321 67

to Boone, NC

Hampton

Dennis Cove Rd

Laurel

Laurel Fork Rd

▲ Dennis Cove

Doe

Appalachian

Fork

Walnut Mtn Rd

Trail

River

Tiger Creek Rd

Tiger Creek

19E 37

TN

143

NC

Roan Mtn State Park

▲

Sugar Hollow Rd

Hampton Creek Rd

Teaberry Rd

Heaton Creek Rd

TN

NC

The Doe River system is different from many other watersheds in Tennessee. Most other streams flow from National Forest or National Park lands where they are protected from development before flowing through residential and agricultural areas. All of Doe River's headwaters, brimming with brook trout, flow through rural, mountain neighborhoods before dropping into the state park, sheltered from development. As a result, most of these small brook-trout creeks will likely be off limits to fishing.

The Doe River is easy to find. Take Highway 19E south out of Elizabethton and follow all the signs for Roan Mountain State Park.

Laurel Fork
SIZE 3-6

Laurel Fork is the largest tributary of the Doe River, and drains some of the most rugged terrain in northeast Tennessee. Most streams that flow from such steep mountains are typically rough, plunging from one small pool to the next. Laurel Fork is quite different though, taking its time flowing at a relaxed pace in many areas. Don't let the long stretches of easy water fool you. The lack of many small drops are made up for with

Tim Doyle with a nice Doe River brown trout.

Wild Laurel Fork brown trout.

several sets of high waterfalls before it joins the Doe River near Hampton.

Most of the best water on Laurel Fork is only accessible via trail, but there is plenty of access for those without a taste for adventure. The stream is stocked with rainbow trout along the road. However, Laurel Fork is better thought of as a premiere wild brown trout stream. In several visits to Laurel Fork I questioned a few local fishermen. To a man, every one of them felt that some of the largest brown trout in the region were lurking nearby. Laurel Fork is at its largest downstream of the Appalachian Trail and Laurel Falls. While this water takes some effort to reach, it is often regarded as the best part of the stream for larger fish. One local I spoke with claimed to have seen a large wild brown trout wolf down stockers as the truck was dropping them in the river. There are a good number of nightly rentals on this stretch of stream that make for a more comfortable stay than the Forest Service Campground up the road.

Dennis Cove campground is centrally located in the watershed and makes for a quiet base of operations for the fisherman eager to get away from it all. This is also the best place to park for a day trip to the waters above Dennis Cove where regulations become more restrictive. Upstream of Dennis Cove, regulations only permit single hooks and artificial lures. Limits also decrease from seven to three fish a day. Browns must be at least nine inches long to keep.

The best time to venture downstream of the Appalachian trail is during the spring hatches of April and May. Don't bother if water levels are high. The fishing will slow during the heat of summer but the fish are still there. Try to arrive early, before the midday sun hits the water. You probably shouldn't fish until dark and walk out several miles in the dark. Copperheads and timber rattlers often patrol trails at night in search of small rodents.

The water upstream of Dennis Cove requires a strong set of legs if you want to travel very far. The trail is rather steep in a few places but levels out when the creek does. The trail has never appeared very well travelled so it's likely you'll fish in privacy as I have on these waters. The long level stretches of water are extremely tough in low water. Most of the stream- bred browns in Laurel Fork spook at their own shadow. Clumsy, sloshing fishermen are the last thing to give them a sense of security. While exceptionally spooky, these browns don't seem to know the meaning of the term "selective". I was disappointed to run out of the current hot fly, but the fish reacted with the same enthusiasm to alternate patterns. Large trout are rare above Dennis Cove, but your chances for a strike are good if you manage to sneak up on them.

Laurel Fork and Dennis Cove are relatively secluded but fairly easy to find. Take Highway 19E and 321 out of Elizabethton. A few miles out of Elizabethton 321 will take a left turn off 19E at Hampton. Take this turn and look for a right turn onto Dennis Cove Road. This is a narrow, windy road that weaves its way between Cedar and Pond mountains up to Dennis Cove.

Little Laurel Fork
SIZE 2

Little Laurel Fork is one of Laurel Fork's larger headwater tributaries. Brown trout share the stream with brookies from Laurel Fork up to a set of cascades. This is a long set of falls that probably drop about eighty feet or so. Only brookies inhabit the stream above this point.

Wagner Branch
SIZE 1

The lowest half mile of Wagner Branch sports a mix of browns and native brook trout. However, large cascades and waterfalls so common in the Laurel Fork watershed have checked the advance of browns. Only brookies swim in these plunge pools.

Laurel Fork.

Northand South Indian creeks drain the mountain coves in the vicinity of Erwin and flow into the Nolichucky River. This area at the base of the western slope of the Appalachians was the scene of America's first move west. Davy Crockett, one of Tennessee's favorite sons, was born along the banks of the Nolichucky in our nation's first frontier. While Erwin can be reached rather easily, it still remains somewhat isolated. Most of the fertile bottom land along the Nolichucky downstream of Erwin remains farm country. Upstream, the big river carves it's way through the mountains, dropping all the way from the slopes of Mount Mitchell in North Carolina. This is superb water for smallmouth bass, and trout are also caught on occasion during winter and spring. Most of the Nolichucky's tributaries are mountain trout streams. However, unlike most other mountain trout streams in Tennessee, the bulk of the water in this region flows across private property.

North Indian Creek is stocked with large rainbows in the fall and winter.

Erwin is a quick trip south of Johnson City down Highway 19W. The only other route from points in Tennessee is to take TN 107 from Greeneville along the Nolichucky River valley to Erwin.

North Indian Creek
SIZE 3

North Indian Creek may be the best small stream that's ignored by a number of Tennessee trout fishermen. The stream drains the fertile Limestone Cove area. This is in the neighborhood of Unicoi, a small community not far from the larger town of Erwin. Most of North Indian Creek flows across private land, but there are several roadside turnouts that are frequented by local fishermen. Excellent access is also afforded by a Forest Service picnic area in Limestone Cove.

As the cove's name suggests, this is a relatively fertile stream for the Southern Appalachian region. Only Abrams Creek in the Great Smoky Mountains can rival North Indian Creek for better water chemistry. Aquatic insect populations are high and complemented by snails. Pick up a rock from a riffle and you will find it alive with aquatic life. Caddis larvae sheltered in sand cases are the most numerous, but mayfly nymphs are also crawling among them. The stream is clear, but the deeper pools have the milky hue that denotes a limestone stream.

Wild rainbows thrive in North Indian Creek and average 6-10 inches, but trout a foot long are not uncommon. However, this stream is kept stocked pretty well by TWRA so it can be tough to know which fish are healthy, wild rainbows and which are stockers in good condition. The area around the picnic grounds is occasionally stocked with some humdingers. You might be lucky enough to hook a half dozen fish between 16 and 20 inches if the hatchery employees were in a charitable mood. Because of its excellent streamside access and regular visits from the hatchery truck, Limestone Cove is a top choice to take first-time fishermen, children, or elderly fishermen that can no longer negotiate rougher waters.

Browns are rumored to hide out in these waters. One local boasted of an 18-inch brown he had caught the previous year and showed me the spot. Most fishermen might look at North Indian and be skeptical, however, the spot the old-timer showed me was a deep slot guarded by a perimeter of tree roots. It was no stretch of the imagination to envision a big brown hiding there. In any case, browns are in the minority compared to rainbows.

South Indian Creek
SIZE 7-8

South Indian Creek is a good looking stream that leaves me wondering, "What if?" Most of the stream flows through residential and agricultural areas, so forest cover is minimal. Because of its current surroundings, South Indian Creek's fishing possibilities are only a shadow of those of comparable sized streams in other parts of the state. In any event, the stream is relatively large and the presence of aquatic snails reveals a high degree of fertility. The stream is shadowed by Highway 19W, and there are a number of pullouts for fishing access. Unfortunately, the lack of cover raises water temperatures in the summer and limits productivity. Smallmouth bass are relatively common, particularly in the lowest sections. This stream flows into the Nolichucky, one of the premier rivers in the Southeast for smallmouth bass. South Indian also has a well-developed network of tributaries, but most of these flow across posted land. Fishing on South Indian Creek is typically best in the late winter and spring following visits by the state stocking truck. Look to tributaries for waters with better conditions and more scenic surroundings.

Spivey Creek
SIZE 4

Much of this stream flows through steep, remote forest. Undoubtedly, this is the best part of the stream and likely the best trout water in the South Indian Creek watershed. Unfortunately this beautiful piece of water is essentially

inaccessible without landowner permission. The lower end of the stream is accessible along a short stretch of Highway 19W. TWRA stocking trucks make regular visits here in spring.

Higgins Creek
SIZE 1-2

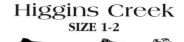

Higgins Creek is a small tributary of South Indian Creek that is easy to overlook if you're not careful. This is a steep stream that falls from Higgins Ridge. Unfortunately, most of the easily accessible water is posted. There is nothing to lose by asking though, so you might gain permission to park at the end of the road and fish the upper reaches of the stream. Be warned, this is wild and woolly country. Small rainbows and native brookies will be your reward, so only fanatics should consider this one.

Rocky Fork
SIZE 1-3

This medium- to small-sized stream is the standout fishery in the South Indian Creek watershed. Like the other waters in the area, this stream flows across private land. However, TWRA has leased access from five separate landowners for

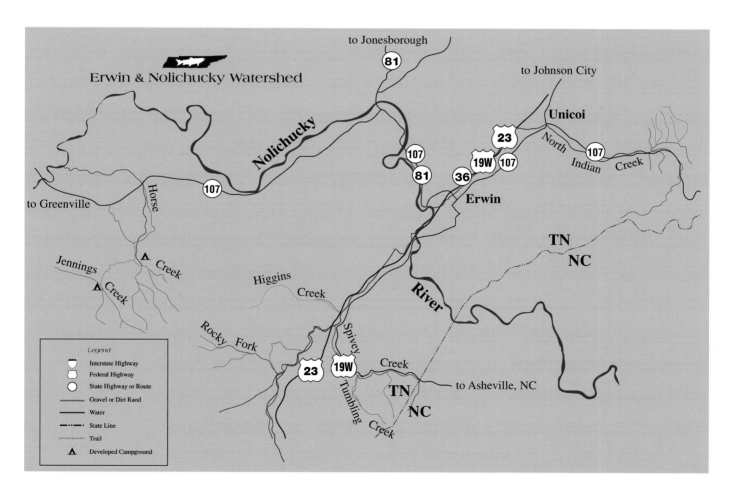

Rocky Fork brookie.

hunters and fishermen. Be particularly mindful of this when you come here and be sure to leave the scene cleaner than when you found it. It would be a shame for this wonderful stream to become posted.

The lowest two miles of the stream flow next to a narrow paved road with a number of pullouts. The stream is rather steep, providing for a number of good-sized plunge pools in spite of the relatively small flow of water. Rainbows are the predominant fish caught along the road. They are stocked spring through fall, but an excellent population of smaller and more colorful wild rainbows can also be caught.

The stream leaves the road at a gated trailhead. Stocked trout and fishermen will become less common the further upstream you go. Brook trout begin to come common as you progress upstream. These are native Southern Appalachian brookies, the lone holdouts from the ice age. Fort Davie Creek and Blockstand Creek are small headwater tributaries that also hold brookies for anyone willing to go that far.

Horse Creek
SIZE 2

Horse Creek is a small stream with a watershed that isolates it from other trout streams in the area. The stream is small and unimpressive as it flows through flat pasturelands on its way to the Nolichucky. While there is less flow upstream where Horse Creek comes off the mountains, there are far more plunges and pools and the creek takes on the character of an Appalachian trout stream. This is still a small stream inside the National Forest, but far more attractive than its downstream flow.

Horse Creek Campground is just inside the national forest and is the best place to launch a visit here. There is a .7-mile stretch of water that is limited to children, senior citizens, and physically handicapped fishermen. The stream is stocked here and makes it easier for youngsters cutting their teeth with a rod and reel.

The stream is open under general regulations further up the trail from the campground. This is small-stream fishing, though, so be sure to bring an outfit appropriate for short casts. Small rainbows will be the main catch unless you find a wayward stocked trout.

Sarvis Cove, sometimes known as the Right Fork of Horse Creek, is a small feeder. Squibb Creek is another stream you may want to explore if you're spending time at Horse Creek Campground. However, these are all small streams and only the stocking truck's contribution near the campground will provide many fish of size.

Signs on TN 107, locally called John Sevier Highway, will direct you to Horse Creek Campground. This intersection is between Greeneville and Erwin. Take it slow and easy on the back roads between John Sevier Highway and the campground so you don't miss any turns.

Jennings Creek
SIZE 2

Jennings Creek is a small stream that has no tributary system. It comes directly out of the mountains and eventually flows into the Nolichucky River. However, this stream is pretty isolated and fishermen are a rarity. Old Forge is a Forest Service campground that is along the banks of the creek and a trail follows it upstream. Small rainbows are the main fare in this small yet attractive stream.

To find Jennings Creek, go to Horse Creek Campground and follow Forest Road 331 to Old Forge Campground.

Horse Creek.

Little River
SIZE 10

Little River flows through Tuckaleechee Cove in Townsend, Tennessee. This is one of the most biologically diverse rivers in the East as it flows from the high slopes of Clingman's Dome all the way to the Tennessee River near Knoxville. Little River is a large yet gentle stream as it flows through Townsend. The state stocks the river with rainbow trout every other week, April through September. Wild rainbows and browns are also present, as are smallmouth and redeye bass. Water temperatures begin to get marginal for trout during hot summers in Townsend, and trout are rare downstream of there. Most of the best water is inside Great Smoky Mountains National Park.

Nymphs and streamers are usually more productive than dry flies. There are large numbers of baitfish in the river, and they seem to be the first to tackle a dry fly. Sparkly nymphs and streamers attract the stocked trout best. Woolly Buggers are easily the most effective streamer, taking both bass and trout.

Townsend is full of hotels and rental cabins. Most of the commercial campgrounds in town are situated right on the river and get regular visits from the stocking truck. Once the water warms to a comfortable temperature there will surely be more swimmers and tubers than fishermen in the river. You'll do best getting out early or late to beat the crowds. Camping is also available at Elkmont Campground on the East Prong inside the national park. While it is generally more quiet, the facilities are not as nice as those found in Townsend's commercial campgrounds.

The main flow of Little River only flows less than a mile inside Great Smoky Mountains National Park before it divides into its three forks where most of the serious fishermen spend their time. The water between the park line and the "Y", as it's known, is composed of several big, deep holes that are tough to negotiate.

Highway 321 is the only road that goes through Townsend. Coming from Knoxville, you may be confused to find yourself travelling south even though the route is Highway 321 North. Coming from Sevierville or Gatlinburg, you will do better to enter the park's main entrance at the

Little River.

Sugarlands Visitor Center and turn right onto Little River Road. You will cross the ridge over to the Little River watershed in about ten minutes.

East Prong of Little River
SIZE 4-10

East Prong is the largest of Little River's three forks, and is usually just called Little River by those who regularly fish it. There are a few smallmouth and redeye in the lower reaches, but the stream is mostly composed of wild rainbows and browns. A few stocked rainbows swim up from Townsend, but are relatively uncommon. Fishing is usually best upstream of the Sinks, a popular swimming hole and the biggest waterfall on Little River. However, fishing downstream of the Sinks can be rewarding, particularly in the fall and spring.

Rainbows are the most common catch in the East Prong, but it is the large brown trout that most fishermen hope to hook. While they are not caught often, there is a healthy population of browns over 16 inches. A twelve-inch brown won't raise any eyebrows here. These are exceptionally wary trout that know to stay hidden when fishermen are out and about. Most of the season, your best opportunities to hook a big one are early and late in the day. Rainy days might produce a better-than-usual brown at any time.

Most rainbows will be smaller than the brown trout. Rainbows average 6-8 inches but larger ones are caught with frequency. Very few rainbows exceed the twelve-inch mark. However, they are usually caught more often than comparable browns.

The campground at Elkmont is a great place to spend some time hiking, as well as fishing. River access is only available via the Little River trail upstream of the campground. However, this is one of the larger backcountry streams, you

*Brian Courtney picks the pockets of the
East Prong with wet flies and nymphs.*

*Author with a better-than-average brown
from Little River's East Prong.*

will find in the Southeast. Browns become rare, but there are still some big ones lurking. Backcountry camping is also available upstream of Elkmont. This is the best way to spend more time on these isolated water. The campsites are numbered and it is necessary to get a free permit to use them. Permits can be obtained at Elkmont.

Fish Camp Prong
SIZE 3-4

Fish Camp Prong is a good-sized tributary of Little River's East Prong, and joins its flow three and a half miles above the trailhead at Elkmont. The waters above this point are lightly fished. Fish Camp Prong sports rainbows and browns in the lower portions. This stream would be a fine candidate to consider taking an overnight backpack trip. There is a good chance that you could have this stream entirely to yourself for several days or only share it with one or two other anglers.

Fish Camp Prong is among the best brook trout fisheries you will find. While the brookies are mainly confined to the highest sections of the creek, they are plentiful and naive. This stretch of water was closed to fishing for over twenty five years in an effort to protect these fish. This is one of the few streams in the park where fisheries managers have experimented with regulations and are allowing anglers to harvest a few brook trout. If brookie populations hold steady, regulations may change throughout the national park. Hopefully this experiment will lead to the opening of more brook trout streams for fishing.

Jake's Creek
SIZE 2

Jake's Creek is a lightly-fished tributary that flows into the East Prong at Elkmont Campground. Conditions are tight, but generally private. Rainbows are joined by a few browns in the lower sections. This is a good stream to keep in mind on crowded weekends, or when water conditions are a bit high. You might prefer a shorter stick on this stream since conditions are relatively tight.

Lynn Camp Prong
SIZE 2-4

Lynn Camp Prong is a favorite tributary of the Middle Prong. This is a pleasant small stream with adequate room for most casters. Access is accomplished only by hiking, but you won't have to walk far unless you want to. Rainbows are the main quarry, but you will find brookies if you go far enough

A pleasant day of fishing at Tremont.

Lynn Camp Prong.

upstream, at least three miles. This stream is the site of the largest planned brook trout restoration in Great Smoky Mountains National Park.

Middle Prong of Little River
SIZE 5

The Middle Prong, also known as Tremont, is a favorite east Tennessee trout stream. This creek is never too big and rarely too small. It always seems to be comfortable to fish and the trout that swim in it are agreeable enough. Rainbows are the most common catch, but browns are present. This is one of those streams that holds a few brown trout that just don't seem to be possible considering the size of the water. Every few years one over twenty inches long is caught by a local fisherman. Fishing is generally best upstream of where the paved road turns to gravel. It also fishes well downstream of there as well, just not as well during the warm summer months. Basic dry-fly and nymph patterns will catch trout with amazing consistency. This stream is a good alternative to the East Prong of Little River when swimmers and tubers are thick in summer. The smaller water isn't as attractive to those wanting to float in inner tubes.

Thunderhead Prong
SIZE 2-4

Thunderhead joins its flow with Lynn Camp Prong to form the Middle Prong of Little River. It is a rough-and-tumble stream of pocket water. Rainbows take bushy dries with enthusiasm. Trail access is good for only the first mile or so up the stream. Access beyond that is only via the stream bed.

Brookies may begin to turn up in Thunderhead after a long absence. Sam's Creek is a tributary which has recently been restored with the native brookies. It is likely some may find their way into Thunderhead's accommodating waters. While Sam's Creek is currently off limits to fishing, keep a watchful eye on national park fishing regs since that may change in the years to come.

West Prong
SIZE 2-4

The West Prong of Little River is the most overlooked of Little River's three prongs. Keep it in mind if you find Little River's East and Middle prongs too crowded for you liking. This stream has an excellent population of small but eager rainbows. There are about two and a half miles of roadside access before the stream leaves the road and heads into the backcountry. While there is no official trail, there is a well-beaten path up the creek. A trail that connects Tremont and Laurel Creek Road crosses the stream at a backcountry campsite.

Laurel Creek
SIZE 2-3

Laurel Creek is a small rainbow trout stream that flows into West Prong. Laurel Creek is small but has good access along

Dan Holloway searches the flow with a dry fly on the East Prong.

the road. In fact, it is easy to confuse it with West Prong. As you drive to Cades Cove, Laurel Creek will be on the left side of the road. West Prong is larger, and remains along the right side of the road until it flows into the back country near the Laurel Creek confluence. This is a good creek to keep in mind if you visit during high water flows. It is usually manageable in everything but the worst conditions.

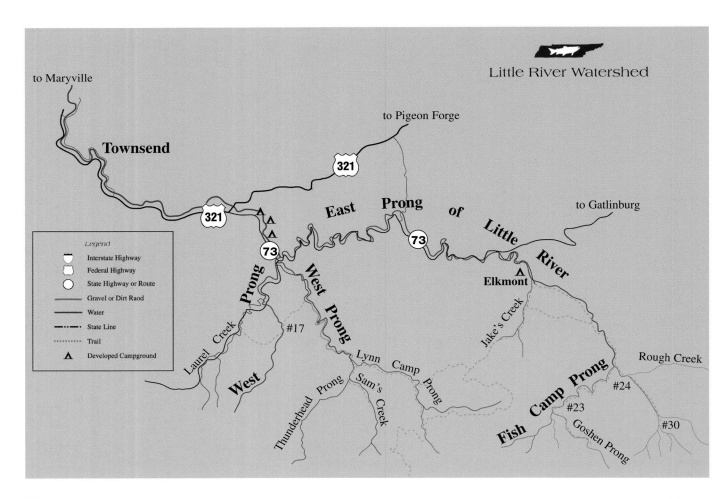

Little River Watershed

to Maryville

Townsend

to Pigeon Forge

321

East Prong of Little River

to Gatlinburg

73

73

Elkmont

Legend

- Interstate Highway
- Federal Highway
- State Highway or Route
- Gravel or Dirt Raod
- Water
- State Line
- Trail
- Developed Campground

West Prong

Laurel Creek

West Prong

#17

Lynn Camp Prong

Thunderhead Prong

Sam's Creek

Jake's Creek

Fish Camp Prong

Rough Creek

#24

#23

#30

Goshen Prong

Middle Prong Little Pigeon River Watershed

Middle Prong Little Pigeon River
SIZE 4-8

The Middle Prong of the Little Pigeon River is often referred to as Greenbrier by locals who grew up in the area. The Middle Prong is a large mountain river that breaks up into a number of smaller streams once it enters the Great Smoky Mountains National Park. The state stocks the river downstream of the national park boundary. In addition to the stockers there are a few wild rainbows and brown trout. The browns seem to be far outnumbered by the rainbows. Unfortunately, this large water outside of the park is a bit too low in elevation to really maintain good trout populations. This stretch of water will fish best in the late winter and spring when water temperatures are ideal. Smallmouth and redeye bass tend to do a bit better in this stream.

The Middle Prong's best water is inside the national park where rainbows are the main catch. The average rainbow will be nine inches or smaller but a skilled fisherman will likely lose count of the number he can catch. The stream follows the road for about five miles and alternates between easy roadside access and deep gorges that require a bit more commitment to fish. There is one picnic area along the river where you can break up the day with a leisurely lunch. If you follow the road all the way to the end you will find yourself at the Ramsay Cascades trailhead. Any fishing you want to do upstream of here will require a walk. The water and the trail maintain some distance between them, but the fishing can be excellent. After a walk of perhaps a mile or less, you might find that brook trout are taking your fly. This is among the largest native brook trout streams in Tennessee. However, because of the population of rainbows, this stream was never closed downstream of its headwater tributaries. Rainbow trout will remain in the mix as you make your way upstream but seem to be a minority by the time you get to Ramsay Prong.

The Middle Prong is best accessed by Highway 321, going north from Gatlinburg or south from Interstate 40. This will lead you to the park entrance and road that follows it upstream. If you'd like to give the lower part of the stream a go in the cooler months, take TN 416 which closely follows the stream. This road eventually intersects Highway 411 just east of Sevierville.

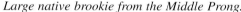

Large native brookie from the Middle Prong.

Porter's Creek
SIZE 3-4

Porter's Creek is the Middle Prong's largest tributary. Large aquamarine pools are bounded by ancient boulders under a forest of hemlocks. Rainbows will be your only catch, but there are some unusually nice ones. Perhaps this is because trout populations in Porter's Creek are lower than other streams of this size. This beautiful creek seems to be taking a beating from acid rain. Soils in this watershed already cause the water chemistry to be acidic in nature. Recent research has shown this problem is only getting worse, particularly after heavy rains. Trout are absent from the higher elevations of Porter's Creek due to its low pH. Fishing is generally good as far as the first foot bridge that crosses the creek. Access from the trail is difficult for some distance beyond. The creek is devoid of fish by the next time you will cross it.

Ramsay Prong
SIZE 2

Ramsay Prong is a fairly small tributary of the Middle Prong. Native brookies are about the only catch here, but an odd rainbow up from the Middle Prong is a possibility. Ramsay

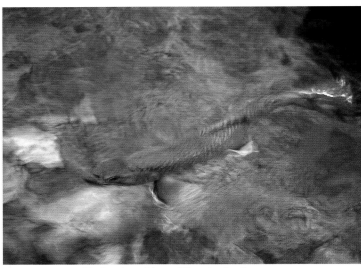

Native brookies still swim in the Middle Prong's deep plunge pools.

Prong is best known for Ramsay Cascades, the highest waterfall in the Great Smoky Mountains. While the walk is pretty, fishing rapidly deteriorates before you get to the falls. Acidic water conditions limit the productivity of this picturesque creek.

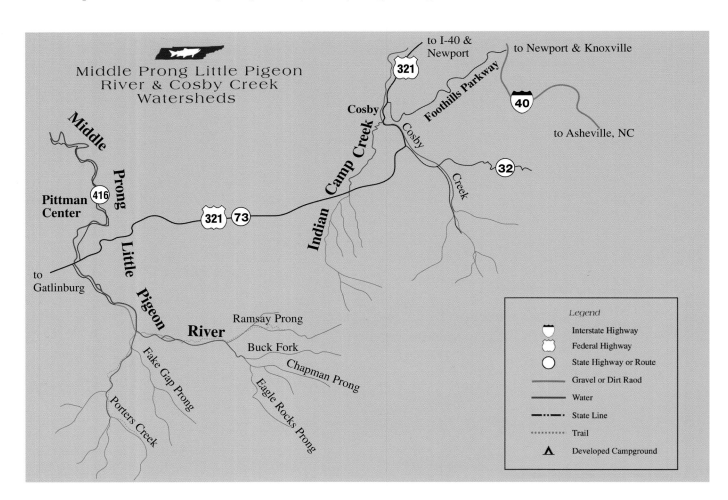

Middle Prong Little Pigeon River & Cosby Creek Watersheds

to I-40 & Newport
to Newport & Knoxville
321
Foothills Parkway
40
Cosby
to Asheville, NC
Cosby Creek
32
Indian Camp Creek
Pittman Center
416
Middle Prong
321 73
to Gatlinburg
Little Pigeon River
Ramsay Prong
Buck Fork
Fake Gap Prong
Chapman Prong
Eagle Rocks Prong
Porters Creek

Legend
- Interstate Highway
- Federal Highway
- State Highway or Route
- Gravel or Dirt Raod
- Water
- State Line
- Trail
- Developed Campground

Freestone Streams
Paint Creek Watershed

Paint Creek
SIZE 2-5

Paint Creek is a medium-sized trout stream that is more or less tucked away by itself. It flows into the French Broad River between Newport, Tennessee and Hot Springs, North Carolina. The stream is named for the Paint Rock, a large boulder near the state line that has prehistoric Native American figures on it. While rainbows are stocked in Paint Creek, it is best thought of as a wild brown-trout stream. Most of the rainbows are stocked in the lower half of the stream and seem to get caught out rather quickly by locals. Paint Creek's browns are a bit more jaded and don't seem to respond as readily to the amateur bait-casters. They do respond well to flies, however.

A massive flood struck the Paint Creek watershed during the summer of 2001. The damage was truly devastating. Water covered the road in most places and several bridges were torn from their footings. Needless to say this has affected the stream. Many of the best runs were washed clean and are now shallow riffles. A Forest Service campground was practically destroyed but is gradually being improved.

While there are some big holes, particularly in the lower sections of the stream, many of the fish will come from potholes or shallow runs. Any likely spot should hold a trout. Most locals that throw bait tend to concentrate their efforts on a few of the biggest pools. Fish will be

Paint Creek is one of Tennessee's only trout streams with delayed harvest regulations.

there but cast at every feeding lane that passes a boulder, log, or notched rock. Those will be the most productive places.

Wild browns will average 7-9 inches, but there are many larger than that. I remember hooking a large trout on my first visit to Paint Creek. Not realizing brown trout were in the stream, I believed a stocked rainbow had slurped my dry fly then retired back to the shelter of a boulder. Playing the seventeen- or eighteen-inch trout rather quickly and roughly, I wanted to get the dough belly off my line before it spooked the whole run. I noticed the red spots on golden flanks just before my 5X tippet broke amid the brown trout's spirited thrashing. If I had a bucket I would've bailed that run dry. I've caught a good number of browns from Paint Creek that topped a foot long, but none as good as that one.

The most private fishing is found by following the trail that begins at Paint Creek Campground and continues upstream as far as TN 70, sometimes called Asheville Highway. The best water in this section is found between the campground and Little Paint Creek. It is much smaller here than where you started. Bald Mountain Road follows Paint Creek above TN 70 but it's on private property.

To reach Paint Creek, take Highways 25 and 70 east out of Newport towards Hot Springs. Take a left turn onto TN 107, sometimes called Houston Valley Road. Watch for Paint Mountain Road on the right. This will access the creek near its confluence with the French Broad. However, this will not be a practical way in until the Forest Service rebuilds the road on Paint Creek. A second way in is to take Forest Road 31 off Cecil Davis Road that intersects TN 107. TN 107 eventually intersects TN 70 which leads to Greeneville. The Forest Service Road will lead to Paint Creek Campground and cross the stream there. At this writing the road down the creek is impassable.

Little Paint Creek
SIZE 2

Little Paint Creek is Paint Creek's one noteworthy tributary. Expect skittish browns up to 12 inches peppered with a few small, eager rainbows. Access is only available via trail. The best way in is to follow the trail that starts at Paint Creek Campground and follow Paint Creek. Another way in is to follow the Appalachian Trail south from Asheville Highway. A Forest Service trail will branch off to the right and head for Little Paint Creek. The trail sees only the rare traveller so this probably isn't a good route for the lone fisherman. Fishing will be better near the confluence of Paint Creek anyway.

Paint Creek Watershed

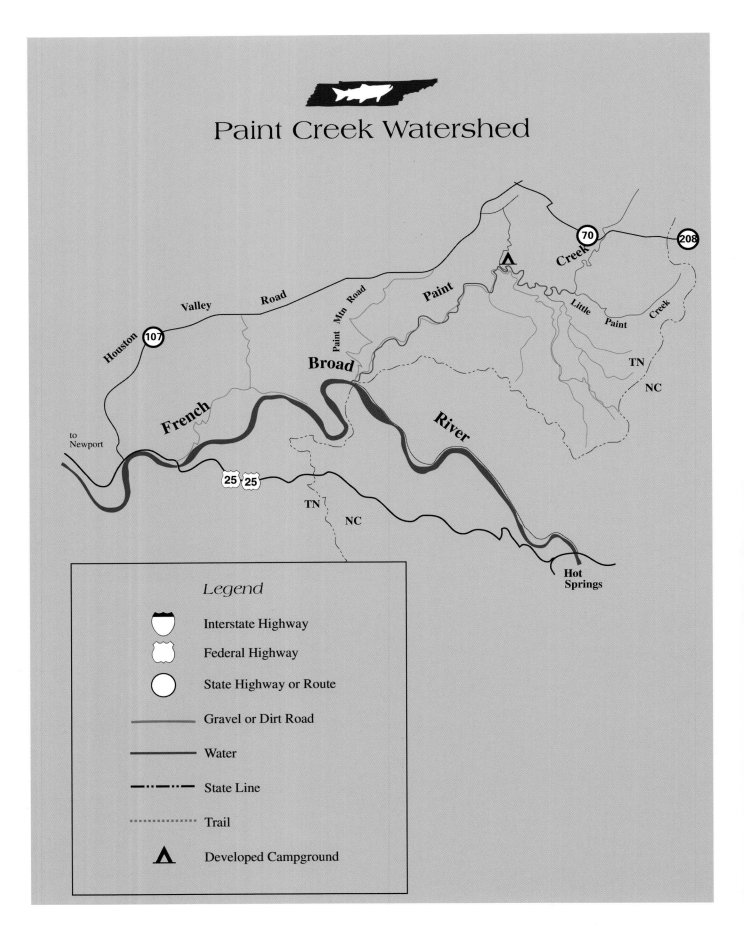

Legend

🛡 Interstate Highway

🛡 Federal Highway

◯ State Highway or Route

─── Gravel or Dirt Road

─── Water

─··─··─ State Line

········ Trail

▲ Developed Campground

Tellico River Watershed

Tellico River
SIZE 6-10

Tellico River is the largest freestone trout stream in Tennessee, and has an elaborate network of fishable tributaries. All of Tellico's trout water is either in the Cherokee National Forest or the Nantahala National Forest in North Carolina. All the best water is in Tennessee as the river rapidly loses size upstream of the state line. Many Tennessee trout fishermen caught their first trout on a night crawler or kernel corn while their elders looked on. Some progressed to using fly rods while others still prefer to use spinning tackle. In order to satisfy everyone's desires, Tennessee Wildlife Resource Agency stocks Tellico River heavily in spite of its exceptionally healthy population of wild rainbow and brown trout. A special daily permit is required to fish Tellico River upstream of Turkey Creek from March until September. Tellico is also closed to fishing on Thursday and Friday during the stocking season. Be sure to check the current regulations to see when permits are required and when they are not.

The very best water on Tellico River seems to be upstream of North River to the North Carolina state line. There are plenty of trout downstream of here but the water can be tough to negotiate, particularly if the water is a little high. Trout are present downstream of Turkey Creek where the special permit is not required. However, this water can be marginal for trout most summers due to high water temperatures. This water can be very tempting for fishermen coming to Tellico for the first time. Smallmouth bass fare much better in this part of the river than trout, though. This part of Tellico River is managed as "Delayed Harvest" for trout down to the Oosterneck Creek canoe access. The river is stocked with rainbows in October and managed as single hook, catch and release until March when special permits are back in effect on the better part of the river. If you are on your first fishing trip to Tellico, wait until you pass the spectacular Bald River Falls before you begin to look for a place to fish. This will assure you're in water dominated by trout.

Most brown trout caught from Tellico River will be wild, since nearly all stocked trout are rainbows. Stocked rainbows in the twelve-inch range are most common, but are sometimes

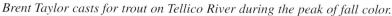

Brent Taylor casts for trout on Tellico River during the peak of fall color.

Brood trout at the Tellico Hatchery.

caught much larger. Skilled fly fishermen will catch more wild rainbows than anything else. Browns are relatively common in the river but the heavy fishing pressure does not agree with their shy nature. Most browns are probably tucked away under boulders during the Saturday morning assault. They are usually caught early or late in the day or during a heavy hatch. An evening hatch of Hendrickson mayflies is an excellent time to see how many browns can be caught.

Green Cove is a small settlement of fishing cabins and RV's well up Tellico River. There is a small hotel here, as well as two small stores. Cold drinks, fishing permits, and trout lures make up most of the inventory. Most of the food in these two stores will be in the best fishing tradition: Vienna sausages, pork and beans, sardines, and crackers are the typical fare, so come prepared if you have a taste for something else. The Green Cove hotel has the only accommodations up the river with walls and beds. Be prepared, though. They cater to fishermen and hunters, so don't expect to find a mint on the pillow. Cushier accommodations can be found down the river in Tellico Plains.

The Tellico trout hatchery is just up the road from Green Cove and is well worth a visit. Concrete raceways are full of trout that will eventually be stocked in Tellico River and nearby Citico Creek. Be sure to see the raceway with the brood stock. These trout are kept as breeding stock and are enormous. Many of these large trout are eventually put in the river.

Tellico's good population of golden stoneflies inspired the Tellico Nymph. This is a top fly pattern on trout streams throughout the southern Appalachians. Dry flies will also catch a good number of fish on Tellico streams. They may catch more trout, but only because more trout fishermen prefer fishing dry-fly fishing.

The Tellico River watershed is well off the most travelled roads. It may be reached from Interstate 75 by exiting onto Highway 68 near Sweetwater. Highway 68 crosses US 411 at Madisonville and continues on toward Tellico Plains. Turn onto TN 165 at Tellico Plains. The road will also be called the

Cherohala Skyway and goes over the mountains to Robbinsville, North Carolina. As you drive along Tellico River, keep an eye out for a right turn off the skyway. There should be a sign directing you toward Bald River Falls and the Tellico hatchery. If you miss the turn you will begin climbing up the mountains and leave the river behind.

North River
SIZE 3-6

North River is a noteworthy tributary of Tellico River. North River is managed as a wild trout stream, with both rainbows and browns. Most of the trout will be under eight inches, but they are greedy and plentiful. This stream also hosts a surprising contingent of large brown trout. You may look at the stream and wonder where they could be. Be assured, though, they are there. Brown trout as large as ten pounds have come from these unassuming waters.

Most of North River is followed by North River Road. There are a few gorges where the river keeps its distance from the road. North River campground is an excellent place to camp for a visit to the Tellico basin. There are also a number of primitive campsites along the road.

As you progress upstream, North River's brown trout will fade away and rainbows will dominate. Hemlock Branch,

Walter Babb holding up two trout caught together on a dropper rig.

Laurel Branch, and McNabb Creek are North River tributaries that are best passed over. Construction of the Cherohala Skyway unearthed acid-bearing iron pyrite that dramatically diminished these streams' productivity. McNabb Creek was the hardest hit of these streams, and its waters are still barren. TWRA has also begun stocking brook trout in the higher reaches of North River. This is an effort to re-establish a wild population of brookies in the main stem.

Bald River
SIZE 2-6

Bald River is the first large tributary you will notice as you ascend Tellico River. This beautiful stream plunges 80 feet over its namesake falls to its confluence with Tellico. Bald River is one of the best wild-trout streams to be found anywhere. While most of the trout caught in Bald River will be fairly small, be assured that there are few streams as beautiful. Long glides and pools are interspersed with pocket water and unnamed waterfalls.

Hiking up Bald River from the falls will take you five miles through the Bald River Gorge Wilderness. This is a lightly fished section of stream. If you have the endurance to hike well into this stream, you will find some truly gullible trout. They are very skittish, though, so don't take a cocky attitude. Basic trout flies will usually produce very well. Rainbows are

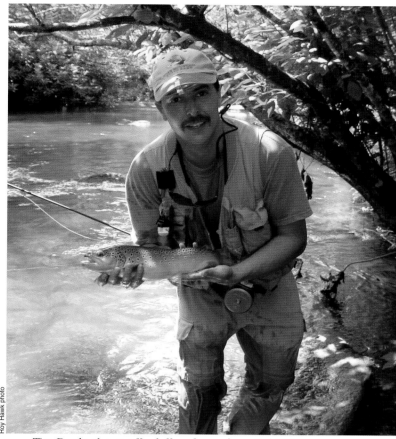

Tim Doyle shows off a lollapalooza from Bald River.

Bald River Falls.

the usual fare, but browns maintain a presence. A few of these browns would even be considered large on the tailwaters.

Backcountry camping is available at several established sites in the wilderness area. Staying at one of these sites is probably the best way to have a shot at one of the large browns that feed most aggressively at dawn and dusk. They are generally open, but you might expect company on holiday weekends.

Holly Flats Campground is situated a little over five miles upstream of the falls. It can be reached by car by taking the first right past Green Cove on Tellico River Road. Holly Flats campground is approximately six miles down a gravel road from this intersection. This primitive campground is an excellent base to use for a fishing trip. Bald River only has about two miles of roadside access in the Holly Flats area. However, this seems to be the best section of the stream to find a quality brown trout.

Trail access is available for two miles upstream of Bald River Road. The stream gets very brushy at this point, but is still fishable for those accustomed to such situations. There is one spot that is occasionally used for backcountry camping. Brook trout begin to show up in this section of the stream. A fifteen-foot waterfall two miles above the road is a barrier to rainbows and browns. The native southern Appalachian strain of brook trout are the only trout beyond this point. Above this waterfall, Bald River has no trail access. The trail follows Brookshire Creek which is extremely tight although it holds

75

brookies. Big-river fishermen will be claustrophobic in this cramped environment.

Kirkland Creek
SIZE 2

Kirkland Creek is a Bald River tributary that has a good rainbow population. This is only for fishermen that enjoy a casting challenge as conditions are tight. The trail is nearly as overgrown as the stream. Nice rainbows up to eleven or twelve inches are a possibility. However, expect most fish to run 4-8 inches.

There is a small campsite on Bald River at the confluence of Kirkland Creek, but you might prefer to stay at Holly Flats, less than a mile down the road.

Henderson Branch
SIZE 1

Henderson Branch flows into Bald River at the Brookshire Creek trailhead which leads the way to Bald River's headwaters. This stream also has some challenging conditions, although there are a few spots along Bald River road where a fly might be cast. Ice storms during the 1990s brought timber down into the creek, and assured a good number of trout safe havens. Henderson Branch has brookies even along the road. Rainbows are also present, along with a rare brown in the lower reaches near Bald River.

Sycamore Creek
SIZE 3

Sycamore Creek flows into Tellico River just upstream of the Tellico trout hatchery. Rainbows are small but prolific in this cold mountain brook. This stream can often be a refuge for those seeking solitude on a crowded weekend. The best way to access this stream is to park at the pull-off adjacent to the bridge that leads to the hatchery. Walk across the bridge and look for the trail on your right. The water and trail keep company for perhaps two miles before the trail leaves the water. There are a couple of good creekside campsites on this stretch of trail.

An excellent population of brook trout has been restored in the upper sections of the creek. They can be tough to find though, since there is very little access to this section of the stream. The trail switches back away from the creek before it reaches the point where brookies are well established. It is

Walter Babb casts to brookies on upper Sycamore Creek.

possible to hike down from the top near Whigg Meadows by following an old logging road. It only provides one-way access to the creek and ends at a campsite on the water. Be sure to have a topo map with you.

Rough Ridge Creek
SIZE 1-2

This is the smallest quality tributary of Tellico River inside Tennessee. Rough Ridge enters the Tellico only a few feet inside the state line. The creek's name should give you some insight as to what the experience will be like. Casting conditions are cramped. However, this could be a favorite stream for the angler hoping to hook a few brookies. The brookies begin to show up only a short distance upstream, and rainbows fade out quickly. Only a few fish will be larger than six or seven inches, but their spunk and color easily make up for their size.

Meadow Branch
SIZE 1-3

Meadow Branch is a headwater tributary of North River.

Historically known for its rainbows, brook trout have been restored to this steep stream. Rainbows are still present in the lowest sections of the stream near North River, but will not be found in the majority of the stream. Only the smallest water on Meadow Branch is easily accessible from a car. Better water is available for those willing to spend time negotiating the less accessible water downstream.

Sugar Cove Branch
SIZE 1-2

Sugar Cove is a pleasant yet small stream that takes its name from the sugar maples that tower overhead. This North River tributary has recently been restored with brook trout. Rainbows still share a few pools and runs in the lower sections of the stream. There is a barrier falls upstream of the road that blocks rainbows from the highest waters. The best way to access Sugar Cove is at the point where the stream flows under a bridge at a hairpin turn high on North River Road. A trailhead is just above here, and the trail follows the stream for some distance. It is probably best to fish up the creek from the road, and use the trail for the return trip.

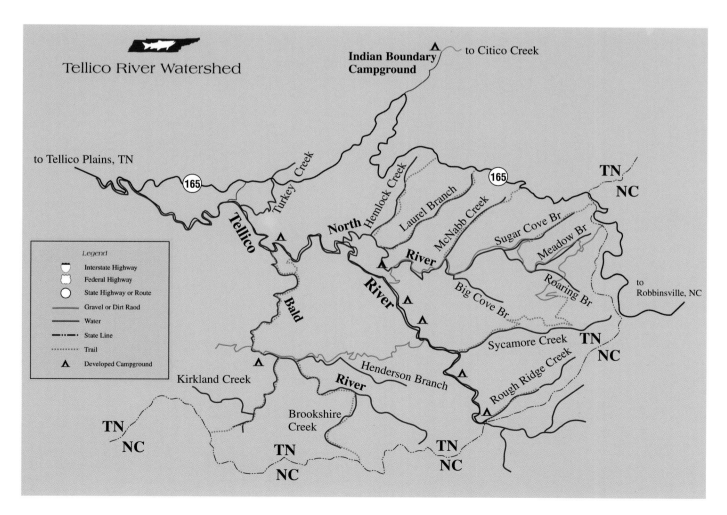

West Prong Little Pigeon River
SIZE 6-8

The West Prong of the Little Pigeon River drains some of the most rugged country in the Appalachian chain. This watershed is located between Mount LeConte and the Chimneys, two of the most prominent landmarks in the Great Smoky Mountains. The river cuts a steep gorge and falls quickly from its headwaters, which fall from the crest of the Smokies.

The West Prong is heavily stocked outside of the national park where it flows through Gatlinburg. This is among the most urban of trout fishing scenes anywhere. Fishermen that choose to fish the river in Gatlinburg may have to fight for a parking space but might be able to cast to the river from their tailgate. Most trout fishermen usually seek more tranquil waters to cast a fly, but the Chamber of Commerce has implemented a plan to draw fishermen. The river is stocked rather heavily throughout the year. An additional permit is required to fish these waters to offset the cost of the stocking. The river is catch and release only during the fall and winter months, and a good number of large rainbows are stocked at this time of year. The prospect of hooking a number of 16 - 20-inch rainbows is often enough for some fishermen to put up with some traffic.

While neon lights, sidewalks, and shopping complexes line the stream in Gatlinburg, boulders, bushes and trees line the banks only a short distance upstream inside the national park. Most of the fish here are wild. They are quite a bit smaller as a result, but a good number of the larger stockers find their way into the first mile or so inside the park. River access is still very good as the stream begins to climb toward Newfound Gap, but a short walk is often required. Any pullout will have a path that leads to the river. This is a classic example of "out of sight, out of mind." The stream is rather large and easy to reach but is not fished particularly hard.

The West Prong of the Little Pigeon is physically demanding to fish inside the park. If the short walk to the water deters you, be assured that this probably isn't a stream you want to fish. The water is unusually picturesque as nearly every pool has a small waterfall at its head. This means that you need to climb several feet after fishing every pool. Fish a dozen runs and you may look back to see yourself thirty to fifty feet higher than the point where you began fishing.

There is a picnic ground along the river a few miles downstream of the Chimneys trailhead. You may begin to reel in a few brook trout in this stretch of water. They will only

Large rainbows are stocked during Gatlinburg's winter catch-and-release season.

A wild turkey just inside the national park boundary.

Tim Doyle photo

West Prong
Little Pigeon River
Watershed

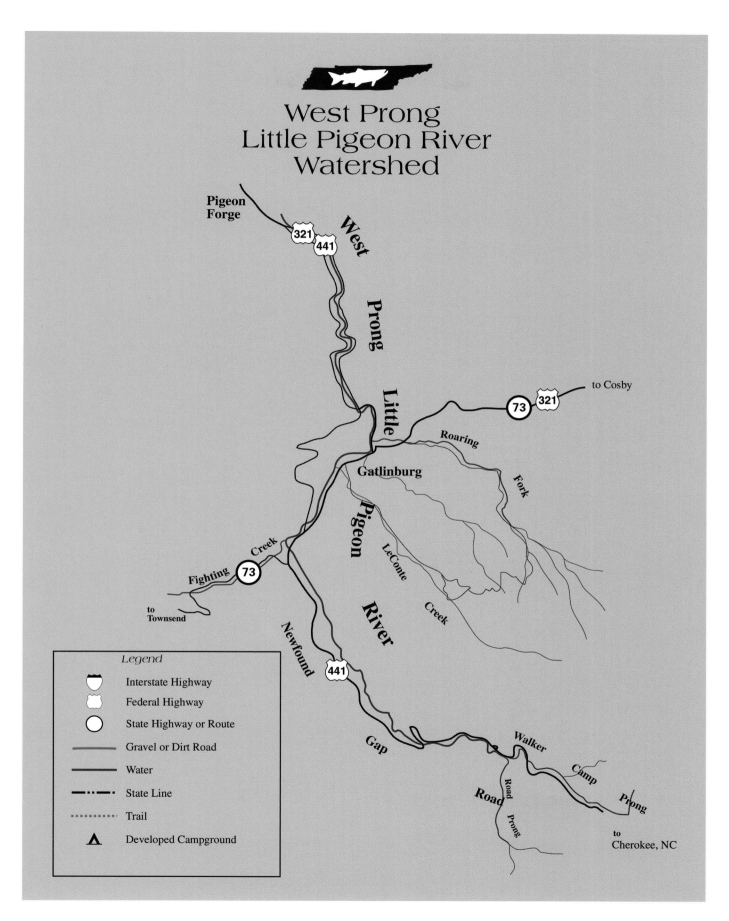

Pigeon Forge

321 441

West

Prong

Little

73 321 to Cosby

Roaring

Gatlinburg

Pigeon

Fork

Creek

LeConte

Fighting 73

River

Creek

to Townsend

Newfound

441

Gap

Walker

Camp

Road

Prong

Road

Prong

to Cherokee, NC

Legend
- Interstate Highway
- Federal Highway
- State Highway or Route
- Gravel or Dirt Road
- Water
- State Line
- Trail
- Developed Campground

become more common as you progress upstream. While this is some great water, you may want to skip it during the busy summer months. There will typically be several people wading, swimming, or skipping rocks. A few hardy souls will fish from the picnic area to a point where the stream joins the road near the Chimneys trailhead. Consider this a wilderness trip because the road is virtually inaccessible from the stream between these two points.

The West Prong follows Highway 321 up from Pigeon Forge to Gatlinburg. Highway 441 through the Smokies provides access upstream of Gatlinburg.

Walker Camp Prong
SIZE 2-3

Walker Camp Prong is a tributary of the West Prong of the Little Pigeon River, but has much better roadside access. This should be considered a small stream, but casting room is rather generous. This is predominantly a brook trout fishery, though rainbow trout are present. This is one of the few streams in the Great Smoky Mountains National Park where brook trout may be creeled. Fisheries biologists will compare populations of brookies in Walker Camp Prong to other streams that are closed to fishing. If this stream's brook-trout population does not suffer any adverse effects, it is likely that all of the brook trout streams in the Great Smoky Mountains will be opened for fishing.

Roaring Fork
SIZE 2

Roaring Fork is a local favorite stream. Very few visiting fishermen find this small stream that is a secret get-away for many. Small but aggressive rainbows are in this boulder-laden stream. Several plunge pools are surprisingly deep for a relatively small stream. Downstream sections outside of the national park are stocked all the way to the confluence with the West Prong. A few of these larger stocked rainbows might be caught just above the park boundary but don't seem to progress much further upstream.

Roaring Fork can only be accessed via the Roaring Fork Motor Trail, a scenic loop road. Turn off the Gatlinburg strip at Airport Road and follow the signs to Roaring Fork Motor Trail. This is a one-way road that exits onto Highway 321.

Fighting Creek
SIZE 1-2

Fighting Creek is a small tributary of the West Prong that flows right past the park headquarters and the Sugarlands Visitor Center. This small stream is typically passed by for the larger West Prong or the Little River, less than ten minutes away. However, any fisherman on Fighting Creek should have its population of small, wild rainbows all to himself. This is also a good stream to keep in mind if water levels are too high on larger streams.

Native brookies still swim in the headwaters of the West Prong of the Little Pigeon River.

Tim Doyle photo

Fishing on east Tennessee's tailwater lakes is entirely different from fishing freestone streams or the tailwater rivers. Without a doubt, it is among the most difficult fly-fishing anyone can experience. It can also be among the most rewarding. A boat is a prerequisite for taking to the water. A john boat or bass boat with an outboard and trolling motor is ideal, but canoes are serviceable as well.

While there are trout in more lakes than are presented in this book, these four lakes are the only ones where fly-fishing, or even light tackle in general, is a practical method. Several lakes like Watauga Lake and South Holston Lake contain trout but surface temperatures are high enough to keep them deep a good deal of the year. They usually stay so far down that deep trolling is the best way to hook up.

Fly-fishing for trout in lakes is generally done in the Rocky Mountains or northern latitudes where water temperatures stay cold enough for trout to prosper so few fishermen think of fishing for trout in Tennessee reservoirs. Locals have long known that trout reside in Calderwood, Chilhowee, Tellico, and Wilbur lakes. However, it's tough for fishermen to catch them. As a result, few fishermen actively pursue trout here. For several years I read every book I could get my hands on that dealt with the topic of trout in lakes. For the most part, these books did little to help me. The reason is that the lakes outlined in this book are not really lakes. Rather, they have a stronger resemblance to a huge pool on a large river. Currents are imperceptible on many natural Western lakes like Yellowstone Lake. The upper Yellowstone River flows into the lake which spills out on the downstream side and continues on its way. This lake is so large that current is only a factor at inlets and the lake's outlet. This is generally viewed as stillwater fishing. Current plays a crucial role in fishing on Tennessee's trout lakes. Most of these lakes are relatively small impoundments so inflow and outflow can cause fluctuations of several feet in a single day.

Three of these four lakes are part of the Little Tennessee River system. Wilbur Lake is separated from the chain of lakes that includes Calderwood, Chilhowee, and Tellico. The Little Tennessee river was originally a cool-water fishery before dams were built. The first dams were built by the Aluminum Company of America, also known as Alcoa. Fontana Dam was built upstream of these lakes in North Carolina during World War II to help generate power for the war effort. Fontana is a large lake over four hundred feet deep. This turned all the lakes downstream into cold-water fisheries. Cheoah Lake is directly downstream of Fontana inside of North Carolina. While it does not fall into the scope of this book focusing on Tennessee, it fishes at least as well. It is an excellent fishery for rainbow, brown, and brook trout. In fact, Cheoah may be a fishermen's best chance of hooking a brookie of perhaps three pounds south of the Mason Dixon line.

All of these lakes are crystal clear. In many instances you can see at least ten feet down. When conditions are at their best the water will have the complexion of a mirror. The margin for error is practically zero. Since the lakes are so large and trout can move freely, blind fishing is not as productive as being patient and sight-fishing.

The trout are year-round residents of the lakes, but summer is really the best time to try for them. Conditions must be calm; even the slightest chop on the water will dramatically decrease your odds for a hookup. The daily fluctuation of the water in the lakes creates feeding lanes often referred to as trash lines by local fishermen. Rising water picks up shoreline debris, mostly leaves, twigs, and pollen. Trout cruising these trash lines are typically keeping an eye out for terrestrial insects that were caught in the rising water or were simply blown into the lake. In addition to eating terrestrials, these fish also feed on midges, caddis pupae, dragonfly nymphs, and damselfly nymphs.

Actively feeding trout cruise the surface watching for food. The clear, still water gives them an excellent field of view all around so getting an artificial in front of them can be difficult. Perhaps the best piece of advice for would-be lake fishermen is to keep false casting to a minimum. The most successful fishermen get the fly on target with a single stroke of the rod. Colorful fly line streaking through the air often spooks these trout. If the fly lights on the water with a whisper you're still in the game, but if the line hits with a loud splat, you might as well start watching for the next target.

The most active feeders behave in a somewhat predictable fashion, swimming several yards between rises. Simply connecting the dots should give you an idea of where to cast to intercept a working trout. Rembember though, there are no guarantees and fish often change their pattern of feeding just as you thought you had it figured out. Most rises aren't splashy, so a sharp and watchful eye helps.

Blind fishing is often less productive, but is still worth the effort if there are no obvious risers. Try tossing small Woolly Buggers in the scum lines, or methodically work the banks. While this can catch some trout, you're just as likely to hook smallmouth bass or panfish. It's not unusual for fly fishermen to unwittingly catch trout on small poppers while working the banks for bluegills.

Off the bow, on Chilhowee Lake in Tennessee.

Calderwood Lake

Calderwood Lake

Calderwood Lake is probably the most secluded reservoir in the Southeast. A drive over the "Dragon's Back" on Highway 129 is required to reach Calderwood. There is absolutely no development on Calderwood's steep, wooded shoreline. All of the lake falls under the management of the Nantahala National Forest, Cherokee National Forest, and Tapoco Power. Most of Calderwood Lake is in Tennessee, but the only way to access the lake is to cross the state line into North Carolina. The state line is about one mile down from the boat ramp below Cheoah Dam at the mouth of Slickrock Creek. Rainbows are the most common catch but browns are present in the lake. The lake is beautiful and inviting but beware, water here is bone-chilling cold. A jacket is recommended any time of the year. Early morning and later evenings are cool even during the dog days of summer. Also, the extremely cold water can form a thick layer of fog on humid days.

The mountains that tower over this lake shield it from most breezes and the entire lake can have the appearance of a mirror. The slightest bad move with a boat can sometimes put fish down longer than you like. Practice your distance and accuracy casting at home not here. Slapping the water with a fly line will not put any trophies on your line. Well-presented flies that light on the water with a whisper work wonders, coupled with a healthy dose of luck.

Calderwood is a fairly small lake, taking water from Cheoah Lake and passing it on to Chilhowee Lake below. As a result, lake levels can fluctuate several feet over several hours. I once pulled a canoe up on the bank at the mouth of Slickrock Creek to take a hike. I returned several hours later to find my canoe adrift in the embayment. Fortunately it was still retrievable without benefit of a swim in the icy waters. Since there can be recognizable current in Calderwood, it sometimes fishes more like a large river than a lake. Current often concentrates feeding lanes along one bank or the other, and sometimes even creates eddies. The current is very slow, though, so it's important to be alert to notice it.

While Calderwood trout are not necessarily picky eaters, they do seem to have an affinity for caddis and terrestrials. Some fishermen do well using Woolly Buggers. However, the real trick is to get the fly in front of a trout without alerting it of your presence.

Releasing a typical trout from Calderwood.

Canoes, john boats, and bass boats all work well on Calderwood. Conditions are excellent for trout the entire length of the lake so long paddle trips are not required. Belly boats are not recommended. Current on the lake will push you pretty far and there is no easy way to get back. The shoreline is too rough and steep to drag a tube a mile or more. Use extreme caution when fog is on the water. Many boaters go far too fast, running blind. There's no worse feeling than sitting in a canoe and hearing a motor bearing down on you in the fog.

Camping is available at the boat ramp on Calderwood Lake. There is no running water but the sites are large enough for RV's and port-a-johns are usually available. There are a few spots where you can camp on down the lake, but the steep mountains that bound the shoreline make them few and far between. It would also be wise to check the dates for bear-hunting season in North Carolina and Tennessee. Bear-hunters use this campground for a base of operations, and their packs of howling hounds can deprive a camping trip of peace and quiet.

There are a few things to consider before heading over to Calderwood. Take a dose of Dramamine on the way because the road from Maryville features 316 curves in just eleven miles as you approach the North Carolina border. Use extreme caution on this road and drive defensively. Motorcycle enthusiasts come from far and wide to challenge themselves on the curves. Any holiday weekend will bring in hundreds of bikers. Tractor trailer trucks also use this route on occasion and are a real hazard to other drivers.

To reach Calderwood Lake take US 129 off US 411 just south of Maryville. This will take you past Tellico and Chilhowee lakes. You might also take the Foothills Parkway which traverses Chilhowee Mountain between highways 321 and 129. The parkway starts between Marville and Townsend ending at Highway 129.

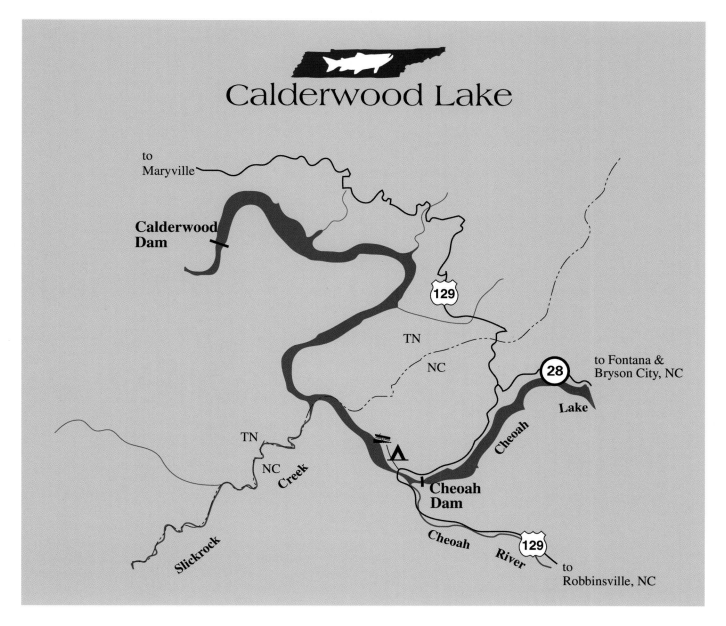

Calderwood Lake

Chilhowee Lake

Chilhowee is an impoundment on the Little Tennessee River built in the 1950s by Tapoco to power aluminum plants in Alcoa. The Little Tennessee is now a chain of lakes starting with Fontana Lake in North Carolina and ending with Tellico Dam at the confluence with the Tennessee River. This is truly a beautiful lake. Much of its shoreline is the boundary for the Cherokee National Forest. There is virtually no development on the shores. Chilhowee is really two lakes in one. The upper end of Chilhowee Lake has cold water thanks to the frigid flow that comes from Calderwood Lake directly upstream. The lower portions of the lake warm up and are a warmwater fishery. As a result, there is a good mix of aquatic species. Largemouth bass are as abundant on the downstream end of the lake as trout are in the upstream end. Trout travel wherever they want from late autumn to late spring while water temperatures suit them. Most of the trout are relegated to the cold water at the top of the lake during the hot summer months.

Chilhowee Lake is at its best for trout fisherman in the summer. The constant fluctuation of lake levels due to power generation forms scum lines in the middle of the lake. Trout cruise these trash lines in search of doomed terrestrial insects, as well as hatching aquatics. Some of these trout are exceptionally large dry-fly targets, however, only the most accomplished fly-casters need apply. Chilhowee's crystal-clear waters give the trout superb visibility so long casts are an unfortunate fact of life. False casting over a trout almost always results in a spooked trout. If you see a boil on the water in the vicinity of your target, consider the fish spooked. Most rises are discreet, barely leaving rise rings.

One of the most interesting aspects of fishing on Chilhowee is the possibility of catching any of several species. Smallmouth bass sometimes masquerade as trout rising in the trash line. There are times when you may set the hook and find yourself latched into a twenty-pound carp. If you throw into a break of shad minnows a trout is likely, but once again, there's no telling. White bass and largemouth as well as smallmouth bass are all commonly found feeding on shad minnows on Chilhowee.

The most important thing you can do to be sure you're fishing in the right spot is to take the water temperature. The cold-water boundary shifts day to day depending on generation schedules. Unfortunately, these dams are owned and operated by Tapoco which is not a public utility. The power generated by these dams is used to power Alcoa's aluminum plants so generation schedules are far less reliable than TVA and Corps of Engineers dams. If the water feels a bit warm to the touch, try to see what the temperature is about twelve inches deep. Surface temperatures warm first and trout often rise up through a few inches of warm water for an easy meal.

A boat with a motor is almost a requirement during summer. A good trolling motor is the most valuable piece of equipment on your boat. Motoring up and down the lake will keep the fish down for good. Canoes are serviceable, but paddling all the way up to the best water will take a while. Skilled paddlers can do well on Chilhowee when conditions are right. However, only the quietest paddle strokes will sneak up on risers. A canoe will be most effective in spring and fall when trout are further down the lake and closer to roadside accesses. Belly boats are almost worthless outside of a few good days in the spring and fall when the trout might be close to the road. Outside of this time frame you're in the bass and bluegill business. Tubes would have a worthwhile application in the upper reaches of the lake if currents didn't dominate your movement.

First-time fishermen need to be aware of a few things on Chilhowee. Always be sure to secure your vehicle and do not leave anything valuable in plain sight. Traffic is light along this stretch of US 129 and break-ins are not uncommon. Also, use common courtesy when motoring up the lake. Swing wide and motor slowly around other fishermen. It's possible that your wake will spook one of the only shots they get in a day.

The best boat ramp to use most of the year is the uppermost one at the mouth of Tabcat Creek. The middle ramp can be close to some working trout in early spring and late fall. The lowest ramp near the terminus of the foothills parkway is best used if you don't mind motoring a bit further to keep your vehicle and trailer in a more public setting.

It's possible to drive to the upper part of Chilhowee Lake near the best fishing. The biggest drawback is that access is extremely limited. The entire area is owned by Tapoco and is used as a storage and utility area. There is a parking area at what used to be a ferry across the lake. In spite of the fact that this would serve as an excellent boat ramp, launching boats is strictly prohibited. Canoes, personal pontoons, and even belly boats can be dropped from here. Keep in mind, though, that canoes are the best suited of the three to get you back.

To reach Chilhowee Lake take US 129 off US 411 just south of Maryville. This will take you past upper Tellico Lake. You might also take the Foothills Parkway which traverses Chilhowee Mountain between highways 321 and 129. The parkway starts between Marville and Townsend ending at Highway 129.

Maryville and Townsend are the best places to stay if you're only visiting the area. Camping is popular along pullouts on Chilhowee Lake. Abrams Creek Campground in Great Smoky Mountains National Park is a more peaceful place to camp, though. Chilhowee Lake is included on the map of the Abrams Creek watershed.

Tailwater Lakes
Tellico Lake

Tellico Lake

Tellico Lake is what remains of the famed Little Tennessee tailwater below Chilhowee Dam. The Little T was widely considered to be the best trout river east of the Rockies and many put it on par with western greats like the Madison and Bighorn. Large numbers of trophy trout fed on heavy hatches of caddis and mayflies. Float fishermen throwing hardware with spinning rods frequently caught brown trout in the ten-pound range. In spite of the river's productivity, the presence of sacred Cherokee Indian lands, the protests of landowners, and the discovery of an endangered species, the Tellico Dam was built and smothered the river. The fishing opportunities presented by Tellico Lake are only a shadow of the river it replaced. However, there is still quality trout fishing below Chilhowee Dam. The vast majority of Tellico Lake is generally considered a warmwater fishery.

Rainbow trout are most common in the two miles or so downstream of Chilhowee Dam. They range throughout the entire lake in the winter, though. Despite this, the upper portions remain the most productive year round.

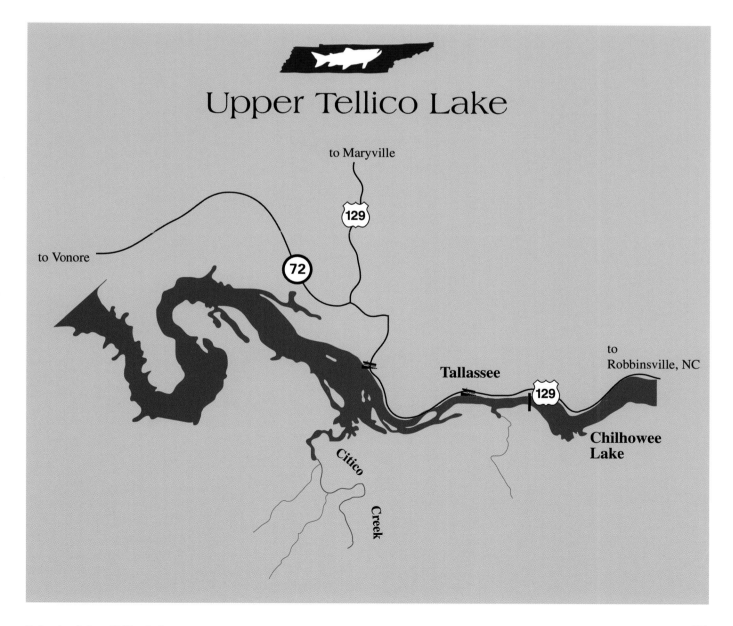

This may be the most productive of the lakes in winter. Caddisflies are present here as they are in Calderwood and Chilhowee lakes, but the trout here seem to have a preference for midges. While the idea of midge fishing might make some fishermen cringe, take heart because these fish aren't usually as picky as trout in the other lakes. Many fly-fishermen keep small flies on hand but rely heavily on size 10 or 12 Black Woolly Buggers. Some feel like the small streamer outfishes hatch matching methods.

The current below Chilhowee Dam is a bit stronger than currents in the upper reaches of Calderwood and Chilhowee so trout seem to hold in one place better, wandering about only when generation is off. This creates the need for a motorized craft, though. The best method is to drift with the current, perhaps using a trolling motor and using an outboard motor to go back upstream and start

Upper Tellico Lake.

Last cast of the day on Chilhowee Lake.

over. Canoes can work during periods of no generation, but there aren't any reliable means of predicting flows. Belly boats are certainly out of the picture. Those areas where current is minimal are too far to reach using flippers.

Tellico Lake is the easiest of the Little Tennessee impoundments to access. To reach upper Tellico Lake take US 129 off US 411 just south of Maryville. Roads are reasonable to negotiate and boat ramps are adequate. However, there are no lodgings on the lake and camping in the trout section is relegated to gravel pull-offs along US 129. Nice rooms can be found in Maryville or Townsend, while Abrams Creek Campground is not far away in the Great Smoky Mountains National Park.

Wilbur Lake

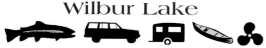

Wilbur Lake is well situated among a number of fine trout waters. Perhaps this is the reason why I had trouble finding many fishermen that knew much about it. Wilbur is the source of the popular Watauga tailwater, and less than an hour from the South Holston tailwater. Excellent freestoners like Doe River, Laurel Fork, and Beaverdam Creek are also within easy striking distance so it's easy to see why Wilbur Lake is ignored by the masses. This lake is probably the most accessible of the trout lakes, but probably the most ignored by fly fishermen. The bulk of fishermen on Wilbur Lake are fishing bait from the shoreline. A few fishermen troll spoons from a boat.

Wilbur is the smallest of the lakes, it's described in this book. Like the other lakes it is less a lake than a large pool on a river. However, this lake affords excellent access to the fisherman since a road shadows its entire length. A TVA-maintained campground is also situated near the powerhouse and makes for a quiet place where you can enjoy a few nights. Elizabethton is only a few minutes away, and hotel rooms are easy to find.

This is easiest lake for fishermen to negotiate. A number of options are available. Half of the short lake is accessible from the road. In fact, I've walked the road and spotted cruising fish.

Running ahead, I was able to cast to the moving trout from the bank and hook up. A picnic area half way up the lake affords some decent wading opportunities. The bottom is firm enough to support a wader, but be sure to wear waders because the water is cold year round. Unlike a lot of other picnic areas along a lake I can almost positively assure you that swimmers will not be a problem. This would also be an excellent place to launch in a belly boat or personal pontoon. Even if there is current you should be able to find a place along the road to get out and walk back.

The boat ramp at the campground is the only spot to launch a john boat and the most convenient place to drop a canoe. Dry-fly fishing is not as productive in this upper part of the lake when the powerhouse pulls water into the lake. However, casting streamers with a sinking line can be worth the effort while drifting with the current. Fish tend to rise more in the lower half of the lake than the upper part during periods of generation. Casting small nymphs under a strike indicator can work better than a dry fly.

There is no place for trout to spawn so all of the trout in the lake are stocked. Many of these fish will carry over from season to season, though. TWRA also stocks large brood trout in Wilbur Lake in fall. The average trout caught in Wilbur Lake will fall between 12 and 14 inches, but larger trout can be expected.

Wilbur Lake is included on the map of the Watauga tailwater.

View of Wilbur Lake from picnic area.

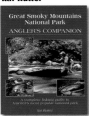